The 10X Rule

The 10X Rule

The Only Difference Between Success and Failure

Grant Cardone

WILEY

John Wiley & Sons, Inc.

Published by John Wiley & Sons, Inc., Hoboken, New Jersey.
Published simultaneously in Canada.

For general information on our other products and services or for technical support, please contact our Customer Care Department within the United States at (800) 762-2974, outside the United States at (317) 572-3993 or fax (317) 572-4002.

Wiley also publishes its books in a variety of electronic formats. Some content that appears in print may not be available in electronic books. For more information about Wiley products, visit our web site at www.wiley.com.

Library of Congress Cataloging-in-Publication Data:

Cardone, Grant.
  The ten times rule: the only difference between success and failure / Grant Cardone.
    p. cm.
  Includes index.
  ISBN 978-0-470-62760-0 (cloth)
  ISBN 978-1-118-06406-1 (ebk)
  ISBN 978-1-118-06407-8 (ebk)
  ISBN 978-1-118-06408-5 (ebk)

  1. Success in business. 2. Success. I. Title.
  HF5386.C2543 2011
  650.1—dc22

                                                                2010052153

Printed in the United States of America

V10002741_080718

*"Anyone that suggests to me to do less
is either not a real friend or very confused!"*

—Grant Cardone

Contents

Introduction

You've probably picked up this book and wondered, what exactly is this 10X Rule? And how will it help me?

The 10X Rule is the Holy Grail for those who desire success. Seriously, if there is an end all, be all—then this is it! The 10X Rule establishes right levels of actions and thinking that guarantee success and ensure that you'll continue operating at these levels throughout your life and career. The 10X Rule will even dissolve fears, increase your courage and belief in yourself, eliminate procrastination and insecurities, and provide you with a sense of purpose that will revitalize your life, dreams, and goals.

The 10X Rule is the single principle that all top achievers are using in the most flourishing areas of their lives. Regardless of how you define success, this book will show you how to guarantee the attainment of it—with any dream and in any economy. The first thing that has to happen is for you to adjust your thinking to 10X levels and your actions to 10X quantities. I will show you how 10X thoughts and actions will make life easier and more fun and will provide you with more time. After spending a lifetime studying success, I believe the 10X Rule to be the one ingredient that all successful people know and use in order to create the lives they desire.

The 10X Rule will show you how to define the correct goals, accurately estimate the effort needed, discern how to approach your projects with the right frame of mind, and then determine exactly how much action to take. You will see why success is guaranteed when you operate within the parameters of the 10X Rule, and you will finally understand the single reason why most people never achieve success. You will discover for the first time the mistake people make when setting goals that, when done, single-handedly destroys any chance of those goals becoming reality. You will also learn how to figure out the precise right amount of effort necessary to accomplish any goal—of any size. Finally, I will show you how to make it a habit and a discipline to operate at 10X levels. And trust me—once you are doing so, success won't just be guaranteed; it will continue to perpetuate itself, literally producing more—and virtually unstoppable—triumphs.

The 10X Rule is a discipline—not an education, gift, talent, or good fortune. It doesn't require some special personality trait; it's available to anyone who wants to employ it. The 10X Rule will cost you nothing and gain you everything you have ever wanted. It is the way that individuals and organizations should approach the creation and attainment of all goals. I will show you how to make the 10X Rule a way of life and the only way to handle projects. It will allow you to stand out among your peers and the industry in which you work. It will cause others to see you as almost superhuman and extraordinary in your actions and your commitment to success. They will recognize your status as a role model—not just in terms of professional achievement but how to live life to its fullest.

The 10X Rule simplifies and demystifies the phenomenon of what success is and what it takes to be successful. Personally, the biggest mistake I've made is failing to set my targets high enough—in both personal and professional aspects of my life. It takes the same amount of energy to have a great marriage as it does an average one, just as it takes the same amount of energy and effort to make $10 million as it does $10,000. Sound crazy? It's not—and you'll see this when you start operating at 10X levels. Your goals will change, and the actions you take will finally start to match who you really are and what you are really capable of doing. You will start taking action(s), follow by more action(s)—and will achieve what you've set out to do, regardless of the conditions and situations you face. The single most important contributor to the success I have created in my own life came as a result of operating with the 10X Rule.

These concepts of goal setting, target attainment, and taking action are not taught in schools, management classes, leadership training, or a weekend conference at the Four Seasons. No formula exists—at least that I could find in any book—that determines the correct estimation of effort. Talk to any CEO or business owner and he or she will tell you that sufficient levels of motivation, work ethic, and follow-up are clearly in shortage today.

Whether your goal is to improve the planet's social conditions or to build the most profitable company in the world, you will be required to use 10X think and actions to get there. It isn't a matter of education, talent, connections, personality, lucky breaks, money, technology, being in the right industry, or even being in the right place at the right time. In every case in which someone has created massive levels of success—be it a philanthropist, entrepreneur, politician, change-agent, athlete, or movie producer—I guarantee that he or she was operating using the 10X Rule during his or her ascent and attainment of success.

Another component that's required for success is the ability to estimate the right amount of effort necessary for you—and your team—to achieve a goal. By using the exact level of effort necessary, you will guarantee achievement of these objectives. Everyone knows how important it is to set goals; however, most people fail to do so because they underestimate the amount of action necessary to accomplish that goal. Setting the right targets, estimating the mandatory effort, and operating at the right level of action(s) are the only things that will guarantee success—and that will allow you to blast through business clichés, competition, client resistance, economic challenges, risk aversion, and even fear of failure while taking concrete steps to reach your dreams.

The 10X Rule will ensure your success regardless of your talent, education, financial situation, organizational skills, time management, the industry you are in, or the amount of luck you have. Use this book as though your life and your dreams depend on it, and you will learn to operate at new and higher levels than you ever thought possible!

1

What Is the 10X Rule?

The 10X Rule is the one thing that will guarantee that you will get what you want in amounts greater than you ever thought imaginable. It can work in every area of life—spiritual, physical, mental, emotional, familial, and financial. The 10X Rule is based on understanding how much effort and thought are required to get anything done successfully. Chances are that if you look back over your life, you'll see that you have wildly underestimated both the actions and reasoning necessary to accomplish any endeavor to the point where it could be labeled successful. Although I myself have done well in the first part of the 10X Rule—assessing the level of effort necessary to realize a goal—I failed the second part of the 10X Rule: adjusting my thinking so that I dare to dream at levels previously unimaginable. I will discuss both facets in detail.

I have been studying success for the better part of three decades and have found that although there is much agreement about goal setting, discipline, persistence, focus, time management, leveraging through good people, and networking,

I've never been clear on that *one thing* that really makes the difference. I have been asked hundreds of times in seminars and interviews, "What is that one quality/action/mind-set that will ensure a person creates extraordinary success?" This question has nagged me to understand if there was one thing in my own life that made a difference: "What *one thing* have I done that made the biggest difference?" I don't have some gene that others are missing, and I definitely haven't been lucky. I was not connected to the "right" people, and I didn't go to some blue-blood school. So what was it that made me successful?

As I look back over my life, I see that the one thing that was most consistent with any success I've achieved was that I always put forth 10 times the amount of activity that others did. For every sales presentation, phone call, or appointment others made, I was making 10 of each. When I started buying real estate, I looked at 10 times more properties than I could buy and then made offers to ensure that I was able to buy what I wanted at the price I desired. I have approached all my business enterprises with massive action; that has been the single biggest determining factor in any success I have created. I was a complete unknown when I built my first company without a business plan. I had zero know-how or connections, and the only money I had was generated by new sales. However, I was able to build a sound, viable business just by utilizing and operating at activity levels far beyond what others considered reasonable. I made a name for myself—and literally changed an industry as a result.

Let me be clear here: I do not think that I've created extraordinary levels of success, nor do I think I have tapped into my full potential. I am completely aware that there are many people who are many times more successful—at least financially—than me. Although I am not Warren Buffett, Steve Jobs, or one of the founders of Facebook or Google, I have created multiple companies from scratch that have allowed me to have an overall enjoyable lifestyle. The reason why I didn't create extraordinary levels of financial success is because I violated the second part of the 10X Rule: the 10X way of thinking. That would be my only regret: failing to approach my life with the right mind-set. I would have actually set targets that were 10 times what I had dreamed of in the beginning. But, like you, I am working on it now—and I still have a few years to correct this.

I mention the notion of creating "extraordinary levels" of success time and again throughout this book. Extraordinary by definition means anything outside the realm of what most normal people can and do achieve. And of course that definition would then depend on with whom or what class of success you are comparing yourself. Before you say, "I don't need extraordinary levels of success" or "success is not everything" or "I just want to be happy" or whatever else you may be mumbling to yourself at this very moment, understand something: in order to get to the next level of whatever you're doing, you must think and act in a wildly different way than you previously have been. You cannot get to the next phase of a project without a grander mind-set, more acceleration, and extra horsepower. Your thoughts and actions are the reasons why you are where you are right now. So it would be reasonable to be suspect of both!

Let's say you have a job but no savings and want to have another $1,000 a month coming in. Or perhaps you currently have $20,000 in the bank and want to save $1 million or that your company is doing $1 million a year in sales and you want to get to $100 million. Maybe you need to find a job, lose 40 pounds, or find the right partner. Although these scenarios cover different areas of your life, they all have one thing in common: the person who desires them is *not there* yet. Each of these goals is valuable, and each will require a different way of conceptualizing and acting upon them in order to attain them. All of them can be defined as extraordinary if they exceed what you have come to know as ordinary. While it might not be "exceptional" compared with what others are seeking, the goal you set should always move you to a better place—or toward an objective you've not yet achieved.

Others might have an opinion about your success—but only you can decide if it is extraordinary. Only you know your true potential and whether you're living up to it; no one else can judge your success. Remember: Success is *the degree or measure of attaining some desired object or end.* Once you attain this desired end, the issue then becomes whether you can maintain, multiply, and repeat your actions in order to sustain that result. Although success can describe an accomplished feat, people usually don't study success in terms of something they have done. They go at it with a mind toward something they are seeking to do. *An interesting thing about success is that it's like a breath of air; although your last breath of air is important, it's not nearly as important as the next one.*

No matter how much you've already achieved, you will desire to continue making accomplishments in the future. If you stop trying to succeed, it's like trying to live the rest of your life off the last breath of air. Things change; nothing remains as it was—for things to be maintained, they require attention and action. After all, a marriage cannot maintain itself off the love felt on the wedding day.

But people who are highly successful—in both their professional and personal lives—continue to work and produce and create even after they've flourished. The world watches these people with amazement and confusion, asking questions like, "Why do they keep pushing?" The answer is simple: Extremely successful people know that their efforts must continue in order for them to realize new achievements. Once the hunt for a desired object or goal is abandoned, the cycle of success comes to an end.

Someone said to me recently, "It is clear you have made enough money to live comfortably; why are you still pushing?" It is because I am obsessed with the next breath of accomplishment. I am compulsive about leaving a legacy and making a positive footprint on the planet. I am most unhappy when I am not accomplishing and most happy when I am in quest of reaching my full potential and abilities. My disappointment or dissatisfaction with where I am at this moment does not suggest that something is wrong with me but rather that something is *right* with me. I believe that it is my ethical obligation to create success for myself, my family, my company, and my future. No one can convince me that there's something wrong with my desire to achieve new levels of success. Should I be happy with the love I have for my children and wife yesterday—or should I continue to create and pour it on in new amounts today and tomorrow?

The reality is that most people do not have whatever they define as success; many want "something more" in at least one area of their lives. Indeed, these are the people who will read this book—the unsatisfied who yearn for something more. And really, who doesn't want more: better relationships, more quality time with those they love, more momentous experiences, a better level of fitness and health, increased energy, more spiritual knowledge, and the ability to contribute to the good of society? Common to all of these is the desire to improve, and they are qualities by which countless people measure success.

Regardless of what you want to do or be—whether it is to lose 10 pounds, write a book, or become a billionaire—your *desire* to reach these points is an incredibly important element of doing so. Each of these goals is vital to your future survival— because they indicate what's within your potential. Regardless of the goal you are striving to accomplish, you will be required to think differently, embrace a die-hard level of commitment, and take massive amounts of action at 10 times the levels you think necessary—followed by more actions. Almost every problem people face in their careers and other aspects of their lives—such as failed diets, marriages, and financial problems— are all the result of not taking enough action.

So before you say to yourself for the millionth time, "I would be happy if I just had . . ." or "I don't want to be rich— just comfortable" or "I just want *enough* to be happy," you must understand one vital point: Limiting the amount of success you desire is a violation of the 10X Rule in and of itself. *When people start limiting the amount of success they desire, I assure you they will limit what will be required of them in order to achieve success and will fail miserably at doing what it takes to keep it.*

This is the focus of the 10X Rule: You must set targets that are 10 times what you think you want and then do 10 times what you think it will take to accomplish those targets. Massive thoughts must be followed by massive actions. There is nothing ordinary about the 10X Rule. It is simply what it says it is: 10 times the thoughts and 10 times the actions of other people. The 10X Rule is about pure domination mentality. You never do what others do. You must be willing to do what they won't do—and even take actions that you might deem "unreasonable." This domination mentality is not about controlling others; rather, it's about being a model for others' thoughts and actions. Your mind-set and deeds should serve as gauges by which people can measure themselves. 10X people never approach a target aiming to achieve just that goal. Instead, they're looking to dominate the entire sector—and will take unreasonable actions in order to do so. If you start any task with a mind toward limiting the potential outcome, you will limit the actions necessary to accomplish that very goal.

The following is the basic series of mistakes people make when setting out to achieve goals:
1. *Mistargeting* by setting objectives that are too low and don't allow for enough correct motivation.
2. *Severely underestimating* what it will take in terms of actions, resources, money, and energy to accomplish the target.
3. Spending *too much time competing* and not enough time dominating their sector.
4. *Underestimating the amount of adversity they will need to overcome in* order to actually attain their desired goal.

The foreclosure issue that America is facing right now is a perfect example of this sequence of missteps. Those who fell victim to this situation were mistargeting, underestimating necessary amounts of actions, and concentrating too intensely on being competitive rather than creating a situation that would make them invincible to unexpected setbacks. People were operating with a herd mentality—one based on competition instead of domination—during the housing boom. They thought in terms of "I have to do what my colleague/neighbor/family member is doing" instead of "I have to do what's best for *me*."

Despite what many people claim (or want to believe), the truth is that every person who had a negative experience regarding the housing collapse and foreclosure mess did not correctly set his or her goals for survival. The number of foreclosures then impacted people's home values across the country. And when the real estate market crumbled, it negatively impacted everything—affecting even those who weren't playing the real estate game. Unemployment suddenly doubled and then tripled. As a result, industries were crippled, companies were shut down, and retirement accounts were wiped out. Even the most sophisticated of investors misjudges the correct amount of financial wealth necessary to weather this kind of storm. You can blame the banks, the Fed, mortgage brokers, timing, bad fortune, or even God if you like, but the reality of the situation is that every person (including myself!), as well as countless banks, companies, and even entire industries, failed to appropriately assess the situation.

When people don't set 10X goals—and therefore fail to operate at 10X levels—they become susceptible to "get-rich-quick" phenomena and unplanned changes in the marketplace. If you had occupied yourself with your own actions—aimed at dominating your sector—you probably would not have been baited by these kinds of temptations. I know because it happened to me. I myself got caught up in this situation because I had not properly set my own targets at 10X levels and became susceptible to someone else's racket. Someone approached me, gained my trust, and claimed to be able to make me money if I would only join forces with him and his company. Because I didn't have enough "skin" in my own games, I was drawn in, and he hurt me—badly. Had I set my own targets properly, I would have been so preoccupied with doing what was necessary to accomplish them that I wouldn't have even had time to meet with this crook.

If you look around, you will likely see that humankind, by and large, tends to set targets at subpar levels. Many people, in fact, have been programmed to set targets that are not even of their own design. We are told what is considered to be "a lot of money"—what is rich, poor, or middle class. We have predetermined notions about what is fair, what is difficult, what is possible, what is ethical, what is good, what is bad, what is ugly, what tastes good, what looks good, and on and on. So don't assume that your goal setting isn't impinged upon by these already-established parameters, too.

Any goal you set is going to be difficult to achieve, and you will inevitably be disappointed at some points along the way. So why not set these goals much higher than you deem worthy from the beginning? If they are going to require work, effort, energy, and persistence, then why not exert 10 times as much of each? What if you are underestimating your capabilities?

Oh, you might be protesting, but what of the disappointment that comes from setting unrealistic goals? Take just a few moments to study history, or—even better—simply look back over your life. Chances are that you have more often been disappointed by setting targets that are too low and achieving them—only to be shocked that you still didn't get what you wanted. Another school of thought is that you shouldn't set "unrealistic" goals because they might compel you to give up when you realize you can't reach them. But wouldn't coming up short on a 10X target accomplish more than coming up short on one-tenth of that goal? Let's say that my original aim was to make $100,000, which I then changed to $1 million. Which of these goals would you rather come up short on?

Some people claim that expectations are the reason for unhappiness. However, I can assure you from personal experience that you'll suffer greatly by setting subpar targets. You simply will not invest the energy, effort, and resources necessary to accommodate unexpected variables and conditions that are certain to occur sometime during the course of the project or event.

Why spend your life making only *enough* money to end up with *not* enough money? Why work out in the gym only once a week, just to get sore and never see a change in your body type? Why get merely "good" at something when you know the marketplace only rewards excellence? Why work eight hours a day at a job where no one recognizes you when you could be a superstar—and perhaps even run or own the place? All these examples require energy. Only your 10X targets really pay off!

So let's return to our definition of success—a term most people have never even looked up, much less studied. What does it really mean to have success or be successful? In the Middle Ages, the word often referred to the person taking over the throne. The word derived from the Latin *succeder* (now—that is *real* power!). "Succeed" literally means "to turn out well or to attain a desired object or end." Success, then, is an *accumulation* of events turning out well or desired outcomes being achieved.

Think of it this way: you wouldn't consider a diet "successful" if you lost 10 pounds and put on 12. In other words, you have to be able to *keep* success—not just get it. You would also want to improve upon that success to ensure that you do maintain it. After all, you can cut your grass once and be successful in doing so, but it's going to grow back eventually. You will have to constantly maintain the yard in order for it to *continue* to be defined as a success. This isn't about attaining one goal one time but rather about what we can persist in creating.

Before you start worrying that you're going to have to work at this forever, let me assure you that you won't—that is, not if you set the correct 10X target from the beginning. Talk to anyone who is wildly, extraordinarily successful in some field, and they will tell you it never felt like work. It feels like work to most people because the payoff is not substantial enough and doesn't yield an adequate victory to feel like something that isn't "work."

Your focus should be on the kind of success that builds upon itself—that which is perpetual and doesn't happen only one time. This book is about how to create extraordinary achievement, how to ensure you will attain it, how to keep it—and then how to keep creating new levels of it without it feeling like work. Remember: *A person who limits his or her potential success will limit what he or she will do to create it and keep it.*

It's also vital to keep in mind that the subject of acquirement—in other words, the goal or target—doesn't matter as much as the mind-set and actions that are mandatory to accomplish 10X goals. Whether you want to be a professional speaker, best-selling author, top CEO, exceptional parent, great teacher; have a model marriage; get in great shape; or produce a movie that the world talks about for generations, you'll be required to move beyond where you are right now and commit to 10X thoughts and actions.

Any desirable target or goal will always suggest something you have yet to accomplish. It doesn't matter how much you've already attained. As long as you are alive, you will either live to accomplish your own goals and dreams or be used as a resource to accomplish someone else's. For the sake of this book, success can also be defined as accomplishing the next level of what it is you desire—and in ways that will forever change how you perceive yourself, your life, the use of your energy, and—perhaps most significantly—how others perceive you.

The 10X Rule is about what you have to think and do to get to a point 10 times more gratifying than you have ever imagined. This level of success cannot be achieved by "normal" levels of thoughts and actions. That is why even when most of those goals are attained, they don't actually provide sufficient fulfillment. Average marriages, bank accounts, weight, health, businesses, products, and the like are just that—average.

Are you ready for the 10X adventure?

Exercise

What are the two parts of the 10X Rule?

_____
_____
_____
_____
_____

What are the four biggest mistakes people make when setting goals?

_____
_____
_____
_____
_____
_____

Why is it a problem to set a goal too low?

_____
_____
_____
_____
_____

Are you ready to 10X?

_____
_____
_____
_____
_____

2

Why the 10X Rule Is Vital

Before we get into how important it is for you to think and operate according to the 10X Rule, let me share a little of my own story. For every project in which I have ever been involved, I underestimated the time, energy, money, and effort necessary to bring my project to the point of success. Any client I targeted or new sector of business into which I ventured has always taken 10 times more mail, calls, e-mails, and contacts than I had originally predicted. Even getting my wife to date and eventually marry me took 10 times more effort and energy than I had calculated (but it was worth every bit!).

Regardless of how superior your product, service, or proposition is, I assure you that there will be something you don't anticipate or correctly plan. Economic changes, legal matters, competition, resistance to converting, too new of a product, banks freezing up, market uncertainty, technology changes, people problems . . . more people problems, elections, war, strikes—these are just a few of the potential "unexpected events." I don't say this to scare you but instead to prepare you for where the biggest opportunities exist. 10X thinking and actions are vital; they are the only things that will get you through these events. Money alone cannot do it; it can help, but it can't do the job for you. If you march into any battle without the proper troops, supplies, ammunition, and staying power, you will return home defeated. It's as simple as that. It's not enough to occupy a territory. You have to be able to keep it.

I started my first business when I was 29 years old. Most people won't go into business for themselves because they aren't willing to take the financial haircut necessary. I had prepared for this—or so I thought—and assumed that it would take me three months to get to the income level of the job I previously had. Well, it took me almost three years to get my business to provide me with the same income of the previous job. That was *12* times longer than I had expected. And I almost quit after three months—not because of the money but because of the amount of resistance and disappointment I experienced.

I had a very specific list of reasons why my company wasn't going to work. I had compiled it in an attempt to talk myself out of continuing. I was beyond disappointed; I was distraught and all but destroyed. I literally went to a friend and said, "I can't do this anymore—I'm done." I made up reason after reason why it wasn't working out—the clientele didn't have the money, the economy sucked, the timing was wrong, I was too young, my clients didn't get it, people didn't want to change, I sucked, they sucked—and on and on.

I eventually realized—after spending so much time trying to figure out why things weren't working out—that it was completely possible that I was missing the answer entirely.

I never considered that I had merely incorrectly estimated what it would take to move a new product into the marketplace at the very beginning of the process. I had presented a new idea, for sure, but it wasn't one that anyone had asked for. I had limited funds, so I wasn't able to hire people and couldn't afford to advertise—which was unfortunate because no one knew me or my company. I didn't know what I was doing and was cold calling other organizations. If this was going to work, it would depend on my ability to increase my *efforts*—not my excuses.

Once I quit calculating all the wrong reasons, I committed to making this work by increasing my efforts 10 times. And as soon as I did that, everything started to change—immediately. I went back into the marketplace with the right estimation of effort and started seeing results. Instead of making two to three sales calls a day, I started doing 20 to 30. When I ramped up my full commitment and aligned the correct levels of thought and action, the market started responding to me. It was still hard, and I was disappointed from time to time. But I was getting four times the results by making 10 times the effort.

When you have underestimated the time, energy, and effort necessary to do something, you will have "quit" in your mind, voice, posture, face, and presentation. You won't develop the persistence necessary to get your mission accomplished. However, when you correctly estimate the effort necessary, you will assume the appropriate posture. The marketplace will sense by your actions that you are a force to be reckoned with and are not going away—and it will begin to respond accordingly.

I have consulted with thousands of individuals and companies over the past 20 years—and I have never seen one of them correctly estimate effort and think. Whether it was building a house, raising money, fighting a legal battle, getting a job, selling a new product, learning a new position, getting promoted, making a movie, or finding the right partner in life, it always took more than what people calculated. I have yet to meet anyone who claims that *any* of these things was easy. Achieving these goals may seem easy to those who are on the outside looking in, but those who know firsthand what it took would never make such a statement.

When you miscalculate the efforts you need to make something happen, you become visibly disappointed and discouraged. This causes you to incorrectly identify the problem and sooner or later assume that the target is unattainable and ultimately throw in the towel. Most people's—including managers'—first response is to reduce the target rather than increase their activity. I have watched sales managers in organizations do this for years with sales teams. They give a quota or agree on a target at the beginning of the quarter and then midway through find they are unable to reach the target, so they hold a meeting and reduce the target to some more attainable figure in order for the team to stay motivated and have a chance of winning.

This *major* mistake should never even cross your mind as an option. It sends the wrong message to the organization—that targets are unimportant and the only way to win is to move the finish line. A great manager will push a person to do more at the risk of coming up short, not target less. This idea of changing targets to make everyone feel good will lead to a further weakening of morale, hope, expectations, and skills, and everyone will start assigning reasons—better known as excuses—as to why the team is unable to attain its targets. *Never reduce a target. Instead, increase actions.* When you start rethinking your targets, making up excuses, and letting yourself off the hook, you are giving up on your dreams! These actions should be an indication that you're getting off track—that you should begin thinking in terms of correcting your initial estimation of effort.

The 10X Rule assumes the target is *never* the problem. *Any target attacked with the right actions in the right amounts with persistence is attainable.* Even if I want to visit another planet, I must assume that the right actions taken in the right amounts over whatever time necessary will allow me to accomplish this. When people inadequately measure the actions necessary, they inevitably start to rationalize. Mankind seems to have this built-in, automatic calculator whose only purpose is to explain away failure. The problem is that the first and most often used calculations always seem to target something *other* than activity level. This calculator tends to be more emotional than logical;

it judges the project, clientele, economy, and individual to be deficient as a means of justifying why things are not working out. This is probably due to all the false content that has been loaded into the calculations by the media, educational system, and our upbringings—excuses like, "the market isn't ready," "the economy is bad," "this isn't wanted," "I'm not cut out for this," "our targets were unrealistic," and on and on. But more often than not, it's simply that you just haven't correctly assessed the amount of action necessary. Regardless of the timing, the economy, the product, or how big your venture is, the right acts done to the right degree over time will make you successful.

I can assure you from experience—after 30 years of building companies and bringing new products and ideas to market—that there will be something you will never foresee, regardless of how detailed your business plan is. I don't care if your product cost nothing to make and it's 100 times superior to its closest competitor; you will still have to apply 10 times more effort just to push through all the noise in order to get people to even know about it. Assume that *every* project you attempt will take more time, money, energy, effort, and people than you can imagine. Multiply every expectation you have by 10, and you will probably be safe. And if it doesn't take 10 times more than anticipated, great. It is better to be pleasantly surprised than greatly disappointed.

If you want to save time in getting your idea or product to market, then you must make sure you do 10 times more of everything in order to be in more places with more people over shorter durations. For example, if you planned on it taking one person to pitch your idea, then plan on it taking 10 people in order to possibly be able to reduce the time it takes. But remember—10 times more people will take 10 times more money, and someone will have to manage those people.

10X parameters allow for a variety of unplanned variables that can strike at any point during a project: employee problems, lawsuits, economic swings, national or global events, competition, illness, and so forth. Add to this list any marketplace resistance to your projects, people being set in their ways, shifts in technology, and, well, you have a whole slew of additional potential events.

For some reason, people who develop an idea about something they want to bring to the market tend to embrace a sense of optimism that frequently causes them to grossly misjudge what it will take to complete their project. While enthusiasm for any project is clearly important, you cannot forget one important fact: Your potential customers are not as enthusiastic about this project—because they don't even know about it yet. The potential market is likely just starting to wrap its head around the notion. Then, too, there is the possibility of apathy—that there will be no interest whatsoever.

I'm not telling you to be pessimistic; just be prepared. Tackle your project with the 10X Rule—like your life depends on it. Manage every action as though you have a camera on you every step of the way. Pretend you're being recorded as a model by which your children and grandchildren will learn how to succeed in life. Attack everything with the ferociousness of a champion athlete who is getting his last opportunity to claim his pages in the history books. And always remember to follow through completely: That is the great common denominator of all winners. They see every action through to completion. Make no excuses, and adopt a "take-no-prisoners" attitude. Approach every situation with an "in-it-to-win-it-whatever-it-takes" mind-set. Sound too aggressive? Sorry, but that is the outlook required to win nowadays.

I know you've probably heard this before, but success does not merely "happen." It is the result of relentless, proper actions taken over time. Only those who operate with the appropriate view and corresponding actions will have success. Luck clearly has something to do with it, but anyone who is "getting lucky" will tell you that their "luck" is directly proportional to what they've done. The more actions you take, the better your chances are of getting "lucky."

Exercise

What is the first reaction that most people—including managers—have when they are not hitting their targets?

_____

_____

_____

_____

When you start making excuses for why you aren't hitting targets, what should that indicate to you?

_____

_____

_____

_____

Fill in the following. The 10X Rule assumes the target is never _____. Any target attacked with the right _____ in the right _____ with persistence is _____?

CHAPTER

3

What Is Success?

know I've already used the term success several times, but let's clarify what it actually is. It probably means something different to you than it does to me. The definition really depends on where a person is in life or what has his or her attention. Success in early childhood might mean receiving an allowance for the first time or getting to stay up past one's bedtime. But that would no longer be of interest just a few years later, when success in the teen years might mean getting one's own bedroom, cell phone, or a later curfew. Success in your early 20s might mean furnishing your first apartment and getting your first promotion. Later on, it might be marriage, kids, more promotions, travel, more money. As you age and conditions change, the ways in which you define success will transform yet again. When you're much older, you're likely to find success in good health, family, grandchildren, your legacy, and how you will be remembered. Where you are in life, the conditions you're facing, and the situations, events, and people on which your attention is most focused will influence your definition of success. Success can be found in any number of realms—financial, spiritual, physical, mental, emotional, philanthropic, communal, or familial. However, wherever you find it, the most crucial things to know about success—in order to have it and keep it— are the following:

1. Success is important.
2. Success is your duty.
3. There is no shortage of success.

I will discuss the first point in this chapter, and the other two in subsequent chapters.

Success Is Important

Regardless of their culture, race, religion, economic background, or social group, most people would agree that success is vital to the well-being of the individual, the family unit, and the group—and certainly to the future survival of all of these things. Success provides confidence, security, a sense of comfort, the ability to contribute at a greater level, and hope and leadership for others in terms of what is possible. Without it, you; your group, company, goals and dreams; and even the entire civilization would cease to survive and thrive.

Think of success in terms of expansion. Without continued growth, any entity—be it a corporation, dream, or even an entire race—would cease to exist. History is full of examples that support the notion that disaster occurs when expansion doesn't continue. We can include the Vikings, Ancient Rome and Greece, Communist Russia, and an endless list of companies and products. Success is needed in order to perpetuate people, places, and things.

You must never reduce success in your mind or in a conversation to something that doesn't matter; on the contrary, it is *vital*! Anyone who minimizes the importance of success to your future has given up on his or her own chances of accomplishment and is spending his or her life trying to convince others to do the same. Individuals and groups must actively accomplish their goals and targets in order to carry on. If not, they will either cease to exist or be consumed and become part of something else. Companies and industries that wish to maintain their status must successfully create products; get those products to the market; keep clients, employees, and investors happy; and repeat that cycle over and over.

There are far too many "cute" sayings that seem to dismiss the importance of success, like "Success is a journey, not a destination." Please! When terrible economic contractions occur, everyone quickly realizes they can't eat or make house payments with cute little sayings. The economic events of the past several years should have made it obvious how badly we all underestimated the importance of success—and how essential it actually is to our survival. It is not enough just to play the game; it is vital that you learn to win at it. Winning—over and over again—at everything in which you involve yourself ensures that you will be able to further expand. And it guarantees that both you *and* your ideas will survive into the future.

Success is equally important to a person's sense of self. It promotes confidence, imagination, and a sense of security and emphasizes the significance of making a contribution. People who are unable to provide for their families and their future put themselves and their families at risk. People who aren't successful can't buy goods and services. This can cause an economy to slow down and taxes to diminish, which will then negatively impact funds for schools, hospitals, and public services. About this time, some will say, "But success is not everything," and of course, it *isn't* everything. Yet I always wonder what point people are trying to make with this statement. When someone in my seminars says this to me, I often respond by asking something along the lines of, "Are you trying to diminish the importance of something you haven't been able to attain?"

Get real! Regardless of whatever goals you are trying to attain—success *is* absolutely critical. If you quit caring, then you quit winning; quit winning long enough, and you will just plain *quit*! Do kids benefit when they see their moms and dads losing or quitting? Does anyone benefit when you can't get your art sold or that great book published or that great idea that will improve everything across? No one will benefit from your failure. However, if you were able to reverse it and attain the goals and dreams you set for yourself—now, that would be something.

Exercise

What are some cute sayings you have heard about success that diminish its importance?

_____

_____

_____

_____

_____

_____

_____

How would being successful be important to you, and how would it improve your life?

_____

_____

_____

_____

_____

_____

_____

4

Success Is Your Duty

One of the greatest turning points in my life occurred when I stopped casually waiting for success and instead started to approach it as a duty, obligation, and responsibility. I literally began to see success as an ethical issue—a duty to my family, company, and future—rather than as something that may or may not happen to me. I spent 17 years getting a formal education that was to prepare me for the world—and not one course was on success. Not once did anyone talk to me about the importance of success, much less what I had to do in order to get it. Amazing! Years of education, information, hundreds of books, time in class, and money, yet I was still missing a purpose.

However, I was fortunate enough to have two distinct experiences in my life that served as major wake-up calls. My existence and survival were being seriously threatened in both cases. The first occurred when I was 25. My life was a pitiful mess, caused by years of approaching life aimlessly, drifting with no real purpose or focus. I had no money, plenty of uncertainty, no direction, too much free time, and still hadn't made a commitment to approach success as an obligation. Had I not had this realization and gotten serious about my life, I don't think I would be alive today. You know, you don't need to grow old to die. I was dying at the age of 20 as a result of no direction and no purpose. At that time, I couldn't hold a job, had surrounded myself with losers, was terminally hopeless, and if that weren't enough, using drugs and alcohol on a daily basis. Had I continued on without a serious wake-up call, I would have continued to live a mediocre existence at best and probably much worse. Had I not committed to a life of success, I would not have identified my purpose and would have merely spent a lifetime fulfilling everyone else's purpose. Let's face it, there are plenty of people living mere existences, and I should know. At that time in my life, I was in sales and treated it with disdain. When I committed to sales as a career and then decided to do whatever I had to in order to become successful at selling, my life changed.

My second awakening took place at the age of 50, when the economy was going through the biggest contraction since the Great Depression. Literally every aspect of my life was being put at risk—as it was for billions of other individuals, companies, industries, and even entire economies. It became evident almost overnight that my company was not powerful enough in its sector, and its future was now in jeopardy. Additionally, my financial well-being was being put in jeopardy. What others thought was tremendous financial wealth was now in danger as well. I remember turning on the TV one day and hearing reports about how unemployment numbers were increasing, wealth was being destroyed due to stock market and housing corrections, homes were being foreclosed on, banks were shutting down, and companies were being bailed out by the government. I realized then that I had put my family, my companies, and myself in a precarious situation because I had started to rest on my laurels and had discontinued approaching success as my duty, obligation, and responsibility. I had lost my focus and purpose.

At both of these pivotal points in my life, I woke up to the fact that success is important in order to have a full life. In the second case, I realized that greater quantities of success are necessary than most people calculate, and the continued pursuit of success should be approached not as a choice but as an absolute *must*.

Most people approach success in the same way that I did when I hadn't committed to it. They look at it as though it doesn't matter—like it's an option or perhaps just something that only happens to other people. Others settle for just a little success, believing if they have a "little," everything will be all right.

Treating success as an option is one of the major reasons why more people don't create it for themselves—and why most people don't even get close to living up to their full potential. Ask yourself how close you are to your full capability. You might not like the answer very much. If you don't consider it your duty to live up to your potential, then you simply *won't*. If it doesn't become an ethical issue for you, then you won't feel obligated and driven to fulfill your capacity. People don't approach the creation of success as a must-have obligation, do-or-die mission, gotta-have-it, "hungry-dog-on-the-back-of-a-meat-truck" mentality. They then spend the rest of their lives making excuses for why they didn't get it. And that is what happens when you consider success to be an alternative rather than an obligation.

In my home, we consider success to be vital to our family's future survival. My wife and I are on the same page with this; we meet often to talk about why it is so important and determine exactly what we have to do to keep secondary issues out of the way. I don't just mean success in monetary terms but in every area—our marriage, health, religion, contributions to the community, and future—even long after we are gone. You have to approach the notion of success the way good parents approach their duty to their children; it's an honor, an obligation, and a priority. Good parents will do whatever it takes to take care of their children. They will get up in the middle of the night to feed their baby, work as hard as they have to in order to clothe and feed their children, fight for them, even put their lives at risk to protect them. This is the same way you must envision success.

Quit Lying to Yourself

It is fairly common for people who don't get what they want to provide justifications—and even lie to themselves—by minimizing how valuable success is to them. It's easy to spot this trend in our society today within entire demographics and population segments. You can read it in books, hear it in church, and see it promoted in schools. For example, children who can't get what they want will fight for a little while, cry for a bit, and then convince themselves that they never wanted it in the first place. It is entirely okay to admit that you wanted something that didn't come to fruition. In fact, this is the only thing that will help you eventually reach that goal—despite the obstacles you'll encounter along the way.

Even the most fortunate and well-connected people among us must do something to put themselves in the right places at the right times in front of the right people. As I mentioned at the end of a previous chapter, luck is just one of the byproducts of those who take the most action. The reason why successful people seem lucky is because success naturally allows for *more* success. People create magical momentum by reaching their goals, which compels them to set—and eventually reach—even loftier goals. Unless you are privy to the action, you don't see or hear about the number of times the successful went for it and failed; after all, the world pays attention only when they're winning. Colonel Sanders, who made Kentucky Fried Chicken famous, pitched his idea more than 80 times before anyone bought the concept. It took Stallone only three days to write the script for *Rocky*, and the movie grossed $200 million, but when he wrote it, he had no money to his name, couldn't afford to heat his apartment, and even had to sell his dog for $50 just to be able to buy food. Walt Disney was laughed at for his idea of an amusement park, and yet now people all over the world spend $100 a ticket and save up their whole lives just to have a family vacation at Disney World. Don't be confused by what looks like luck to you. Lucky people don't make successful people; people who completely commit themselves to success seem to get lucky in life. Someone once said, "The harder I work, the luckier I get."

We can even take this one step further: If you are able to repeatedly attain success, it becomes less of a "success" and more of a habit—almost everyday life for some people. Successful people have even been described as having a certain magnetism—some "x factor" or magical charm that seems to surround and follow them. Why? Because successful individuals approach success as a duty, obligation, and responsibility—and even a right! Let's say that there's an opportunity for success in the vicinity of two people. Do you think it will end up with the person who believes success is his or her duty—who reaches out and grabs it—or the one who approaches it with a "take-it-or-leave-it" attitude? I think you know the answer.

And despite the oft-used phrase, there is no such thing as an "overnight success." Success always comes as a result of earlier actions—no matter how seemingly insignificant they are or how long ago they were taken. Anyone who refers to a business, product, actor, or band as an overnight success neglects to understand the mental stakes that certain individuals have made in order to forge this path. They don't see the countless actions taken before these people actually created and acquired their much-deserved victory.

Success comes about as a result of mental and spiritual claims to own it, followed by taking necessary actions over time until it is acquired. If you approach it with any less gusto than your ethical and moral duty, obligation, and responsibility to your family, your company, and your future, you will most likely not create it—and have even more difficulty keeping it.

I guarantee that when you, your family, and your company begin to consider success to be a responsibility and an ethical issue, then everything else will immediately start to shift. Although ethics are certainly a personal issue, most people would agree that being ethical is not necessarily limited to telling the truth or not stealing money. Our definition of ethics can certainly be expanded from that—perhaps even to include the notion that we are required to live up to the potential with which we've each been blessed. I even suggest that failing to insist upon abundant amounts of success is somewhat unethical. To the degree that electing to do our personal best each and every day is ethical, then failing to do so is a violation of ethics.

You must constantly demand success as your duty, obligation, and responsibility. I am going to show you how to guarantee that this happens—in any business or industry, at any time, despite all obstacles, and in whatever volumes you desire!

Success must be approached from an ethical viewpoint. Success is your duty, obligation, and responsibility!

Exercise

Success should be approached as your _____,
_____, and _____.

Write in your own words how success is your duty, obligation, and responsibility.

_____

_____

_____

_____

_____

_____

Write two examples of how you lie to yourself about success.

_____

_____

_____

_____

_____

What are two things that are important to know about success?

_____

_____

_____

_____

_____

5

There Is No Shortage of Success

The way you view success is just as important as how you approach success. Unlike a product that is manufactured and inventoried, there is no "limit" as to how much success can be created. You can have as much as you want, and so can I—and your achievement does not prevent or limit my ability to achieve. Unfortunately, most people look at success as though it is somehow a scarcity. They tend to think that if someone else is successful, it will somehow inhibit their ability to create success. Success is not a lottery, bingo, a horse race, or a card game that allows for only one winner. It is simply not the case. Gordon Gekko in the movie *Wall Street* said, "for every winner, there is a loser." Success is not a zero sum game, there can be many winners. Success is not a commodity or resource that has limited reserves.

There will never be a dearth of success because it is created by those who have no limits in terms of ideas, creativity, ingenuity, talent, intelligence, originality, persistence, and determination. Notice that I refer to success as something that's *created*—not *acquired*. Unlike copper, silver, gold, or diamonds—items that already exist and that you must find in order to bring to market—success is something people *make*. Great ideas, new technologies, innovative products, and fresh solutions to old problems are all things that will never exist in shortages. The creation of success can take place all over the world—either at the same time or at different times and at different levels—by millions of people who have no limits. Success doesn't depend on resources or supplies or space.

Politics and the media perpetuate these shortage concepts by suggesting that there is not "enough" of certain things to go around—that "if you have something, I cannot." Many politicians believe they need to spread this myth in order to energize their followers to take a stand for or against another politician or party. They make statements like, "I will take better care of you than the other guy," "I will make life easier for you," "I will reduce taxes for you," "I promise better education for your kids," or "I will make it more possible for you to be successful." The underlying implication of these claims is that only *I* can do this—not the other guy. These politicians first emphasize the topics and initiatives that they know followers consider important—then they create the sense that citizens aren't capable of doing things for themselves. They highlight the "scarcity" that exists and do their best to make people feel that their only chance of getting what they want and need is to support them. Otherwise, they imply, your chances of getting your share become even *more* remote.

One of the reasons why it's difficult to discuss politics or religion with people is because exchanges about both tend to suggest a shortage—which then causes inevitable disputes. For example, if your political beliefs win, then my politics lose. If one party gets what it supports, then another group must suffer. The same can be said for certain general attitudes and viewpoints. It's extremely difficult for people to "agree to disagree";

people operate under the assumption that one person's beliefs cannot be maintained if another person's conflicting beliefs exist. This notion—based once again on the concept of limits and shortages—only increases the amount of tension we have with one another. Why does one person have to be wrong and another right? Why the need for shortages?

The notion of competition suggests that if one person wins, someone else must lose. Although this might be true in a board game, where the goal is to produce one winner, this is not the reality with regard to success in business and in life. The big players do not think in terms of restrictions like this. Instead, they think without limits—something that allows them to soar to levels that many others consider impossible. Financial legend Warren Buffett's success is not capped or limited because of someone *else's* investment strategies, and in no way does his financial prowess confine or limit *my* ability to create financial success for myself. The founders of Google didn't stop the creation of Facebook, nor did two decades of Microsoft's dominance prevent Steve Jobs from raising Apple's profile with iPods, iPhones, and iPads. Similarly, the amount of new products, ideas, and successful creations by these companies over the past few years will not prevent others—maybe you—from generating success at even more astounding magnitudes.

You don't have to look far to see the shortage myth perpetuated by most of the population via expressions of envy, disagreement, unfairness, and suggestions that those who "hit it big" have been unfairly compensated. Then there are the constant reports in the media of shortages of jobs, money, opportunities, and even time. How often do you hear someone make the claim that "there isn't enough time in the day"? Or someone else complain that "there aren't any good jobs" or that "no one is hiring." The reality is that even if 20 percent of the population is unemployed, 80 percent have jobs.

Another example of this "shortage thinking" has taken place right in my own neighborhood. The man who lives next door to me is, incidentally, one of the most famous actors in Hollywood; he's a major star and an incredible actor. The road that separates my house from his constantly has pot- holes that the city never seems to be able to fix. Another neighbor who lives at the end of the street had the gall to suggest that "the movie star" fix the street because he makes $20 million a movie. I was shocked by this person's thought process regarding success—that just because this actor had created success beyond that which any of us in the neighbor- hood had, he should foot the bill for fixing the street. I was thinking that the rest of us should improve the road for him, since he improves the value of our neighborhood!

When some TV personality gets a massive financial contract, people often react by asking, "How can one person get paid so much money?" But money is created by man and printed by machines. Not even money exists in shortages; it merely suffers from reductions in value. Some group deeming a single individual worth $400 million should be an encour- agement to you that *anything* is possible.

I've found that most—if not all—shortages are simply manufactured notions. The company or organization that can convince you that there are limited amounts of whatever you need or want—be it diamonds, oil, water, clean air, cool weather, warm weather, energy—can produce a sense of urgency, thereby inspiring people to support their cause.

You must rid yourself of the concept that success can be restricted in any way. Operating under this notion will hurt your ability to create success for yourself. Let's say that you and I are bidding to win a client, and I get the business. This doesn't mean that you cannot be successful; after all, this wasn't the only client you were bidding for. Being dependent on only a single thing or person for success will limit your chances of achievement. Although you and I are competing on this one contract, "Mr. Think Big—No Shortages" is win- ning thousands of clients and showing us the *real* definition of success!

To get beyond the shortage myth, you have to shift your thinking to see that others' achievements actually create an opportunity for you to win as well. *Success for anyone or any group is ultimately a positive contribution to all people and all groups as it provides validation of the possibilities to all.* That is why people become so inspired when they witness some great victory or performance. Seeing success in action invigorates us all and reduces our belief that our ability to accomplish something is "impossible." Whether the success is new technology, a medical breakthrough, a higher score, a faster time, or a new record price for a business acquisition—and whether you participated or not—achievements like these are a confirmation that success is not in shortage and is entirely possible for anyone.

Erase any concepts you might have that success is limited only to some and only in certain amounts. You and I can get as much as we want—at the same time. The moment you start thinking someone else's gain is your loss, you limit yourself by thinking in terms of competition and shortages. This is the moment when you must discipline your thinking to equate any success with the possibilities for more success. Then move back to your commitment that success is your ethical duty. This will motivate the most creative parts of you to find the solution and the way in which you can create original success in abundant amounts.

Exercise

Write down an example of shortages of success that you have seen.

_____
_____
_____
_____
_____
_____
_____

How are so-called shortages actually created?

_____
_____
_____
_____
_____
_____

There exist no shortages of success, but what is there truly a shortage of?

_____
_____
_____
_____
_____
_____
_____

6

Assume Control for Everything

I was going to call this chapter "Don't Be a Little Bitch" but decided to back off a bit so as not to offend anyone. I have been trying to work this title in since I published my last book, *If You're Not First, You're Last*. I still love the title and have been dying to work it in somewhere. I thought it would be perfect for this chapter, since the purpose here is to discuss the idea that crybabies, whiners, and victims just don't do well at attracting or creating success. It's not even that they aren't capable; it's just that people who typically succeed are required to take big actions—and it is impossible to take big actions if you don't take responsibility. It is equally impossible to do something positive when you are spending your time making excuses.

You must understand—as I've already stated countless times—that success is not something that happens *to* you;

it's something that happens *because* of you and because of the actions you take. People who refuse to take responsibility generally don't do well at taking much action and subsequently don't do well in the game of success. Successful people accept very high levels of accountability for creating and having success for themselves—and even for failing to do so. Successful people hate the blame game and know that it is better to make something happen—good *or* bad—than to have it happen to you.

Those who suffer from victim thinking—which I roughly estimate to be about 50 percent of the population—will hate this chapter and probably picked up this book by mistake. Anyone who uses blame as the reason why something happened or did not happen will never accumulate real success in life and only further his or her status as a slave on this planet. Those who give control over to another for their success—or lack of it—will never be in control of their lives. No game in life is truly enjoyable without first accepting control over your understanding of the game, how you play the game, and then the outcome of the game. People who assume the position of victim will never be secure—simply because they elect to turn over responsibility to another party and because they never elect to *know* for themselves what they can do. They therefore never take charge over their outcomes going forward, saying, "I am a little victim; bad things happen to me often, and I cannot do anything about it."

To get where you want to go in life, you must adopt the view that *whatever* is going on in your world—good, bad, or nothing—is something caused by *you*. I assume control over everything that happens to me, even for those things that I appear to have no control over. Whether I am in control or not, I still elect to claim responsibility and control so that I can do something to improve my situation going forward. If, for example, the electricity goes out in my neighborhood, rather than blaming the city or the state for blackouts, I look at what I could do differently in order not to be impacted negatively the next time this happens. Do *not* confuse this with some compulsive need for control; rather, it's simply a high-level, healthy sense of responsibility and a way for me to generate effective solutions. The reality is that I didn't have anything to do with the lights going out; it could have been due to too many people using electricity at the same time, heat waves, weather, an earthquake, or someone hitting a transformer. I paid my bill as scheduled, and now I am without electricity and heat and am unable to boil water, refrigerate food, or use my computers. Blaming won't change any of those conditions, and because success is my duty, obligation, and responsibility, it is a bit hard for me now to turn that over to the state. It is kind of hard to consider yourself successful if you are without lights, heat, or unspoiled foods.

When I assume and increase my responsibility for this situation, I will probably come up with a solution going forward. You have probably already thought of what it could be. This didn't just happen to me because the electricity went out. It happened to me because I didn't have a backup generator. This wasn't bad luck or even bad planning; it was the result of turning responsibility over to someone else. Don't be a little bitch—get a generator. Oh, but generators cost money! Not as much money as being without electricity for three days and not being able to take care of your family. Once you decide to take control and increase responsibility, you will start to find successful solutions to making your life better!

Assume control and increase responsibility by adopting the position that you make all things happen, even those things you have previously considered to not be under your control. Never take the position that things just happen to you; rather, they happen because of something you did or did not do. If you are willing to take credit when you win, you have to take credit when you don't! Increasing your responsibility level will inherently enhance your ability to find solutions and create more success for yourself. Blaming someone or something else only extends how long you will be a victim and slave. Assuming control will cause you to start to look at what you can do to make sure negative events don't take place so that you can improve the quality of your life and reduce the occurrence of seemingly random unfortunate events.

Let's say that someone rear-ends me. Clearly, that person is at fault. Although I will be upset with him or her, the last thing I want to do is assume the position of victim. How horrible! "Look what happened to me—oh, poor me—I am a victim." Would you get a business card or have a television campaign stating this to the public as a way to garner respect and attention? Of course not! Never claim the position of victim after deciding to create a life filled with success. Instead, figure out how to reduce the chances of inconveniences, like people rear-ending you, from ever happening again.

The 10X Rule refers to massive amounts of action taken persistently over time. In order to make good things happen more often, you cannot afford to act like a victim. Good things don't happen to victims; bad things do—quite frequently—and all you have to do is ask them. Those who embrace the victim position will gladly go on and on to you about how they had nothing to do with their many bad breaks and misfortunes in life that seem to strike them time and again throughout their lives. There are four consistent factors in the life of the victim: (1) bad things happen to them, (2) bad things happen often, (3) they are always involved, and (4) someone or something else is always to blame.

Successful people take the opposite stance, and you must too: Everything that happens in your life comes as a result of your own responsibility, not merely some outside force. This will prompt you to start looking for ways to move beyond the situation and take control of not having bad things "happen" to you in the future. Begin to ask yourself after every unpleasant encounter or event, "What can I do to reduce my chances of it happening again—or even ensure that it doesn't happen again?" Returning to my earlier example of being rear-ended: There are so many ways you might have prevented yourself from having a distracted driver run into the back of your car. You could have gotten a driver, left earlier or later, closed the deal last week, taken a different route—or been so important that your clients would have driven to you rather than you to them.

Let me try to get you to shift your thinking just a bit more before I move on. Many people agree with the notion that you draw or attract into your life the things—and people—to which you pay the most attention. Many may also agree that they have tapped into only a small portion of their understanding and mental capability. Is there any possibility, then, that you made some decision that you might not have even be aware of sometime prior to your appointment to, in a sense, create this supposed accident so that you could continue to have something to blame for your life? If it is even remotely possible, it is worth investigating! Understand that you had to be at that one place at that perfect moment in order to be in the accident. Thousands of other people were not involved—you were. You left at the precise time to coordinate with someone on one of a hundred streets and then arranged to be at that exact spot, at that precise moment, and positioned yourself directly in front of that one special driver who was not paying attention and rammed into your car. When bad things happen to good people, I assure you that the good people had more to do with it than they take responsibility for.

Had you left just moments earlier, you could have avoided the supposed accident. Had you been driving at any other speed, it would have been impossible for you to have coordinated so perfectly. Had you taken any other street, it would not have happened. Sound too far out there? Was it just an accident and just bad luck? Maybe you are just a victim, destined to a life of bad luck and misfortune. When the physical universe keeps slapping you around and it's not getting any better, you may want to consider that things happen not just by luck and happenstance but that you have *something* to do with what is happening—or it would not have involved you.

Remember, although it may be happening to you, it is happening because of you. Although you may not want to claim responsibility for the accident on the police report, the reality is that the insurance company is going to exact a penalty regardless of who is at fault. Keep one thing in mind: Anytime you play victim in order to "be right," you are taking on the identity of a victim, and that can't be a good thing. Until a person is done being a victim, he or she is unable to create solutions and success. That person only has problems.

Once you start to approach every situation as someone who is *acting*—not being *acted upon*—you will start to have more control over your life. Having (or failing to have) success, I believe, is a direct result of everything you are doing and thinking yourself. *You* are the source, the generator, the origin, and the reason for everything—both positive and negative. This is not meant to simplify the concept of success, of course, but until you decide you are responsible for everything, you likely will not take the action necessary to get you above the game. However, if you want to have it all, then of course you have to assume responsibility for everything. Otherwise, you are going to waste a lot of potential 10X energy making excuses instead of profits.

It is a myth and falsehood to think that success just happens or that it just happens to some people. I know that the approach I'm suggesting works, because it's the one I've used to accumulate my own success. I didn't grow up in an especially privileged household with any connections to the supposedly "right" people. I was given no money to start my companies and was not especially more "gifted" than the next person. Yet I was able to accumulate financial, physical, spiritual, and emotional success that is far beyond anything most people expected of me—all because I was willing to take actions at massive levels, assume control, and take responsibility for every outcome. Whether it is the flu, a stomachache, a car wreck, a criminal stealing my money, my computer crashing, or even the electricity going out, I assume control and responsibility.

It was only until I truly started to believe that *nothing happens to me; it happens because of me* that I was able to start operating at 10X levels. Someone once said, "No matter where I go, there I am." This little saying suggested to me that I am both the problem and the solution. This outlook put me in a position of being the cause of the outcomes of my life rather than a victim. I didn't allow myself to blame anyone or anything else as a justification for any hardships I encountered. I started to believe that although I may not always have a say in what happens to me, I *always* have a choice about how I respond to it. Success isn't just a "journey," as countless people and books suggest it is; rather, it's a state—constant or otherwise—over which you have control and responsibility. You either create success or you don't—and it isn't for whiners, crybabies, and victims.

You doubtlessly have gifts you have yet to use—potential that remains untapped. You've been endowed with a desire for greatness and are aware enough to know that there are no shortages of success. Increase your responsibility level, assume control for everything that happens to you, and live by the slogan that nothing happens to you—only because of you! And remember, "Don't be a little bitch."

Exercise

What do you want to assume control of in your life?

_____

_____

_____

_____

_____

_____

Success is not something that happens _to_ you; it's something that happens _____.

Write three examples when you made success happen, it didn't just happen to you.

_____

_____

_____

_____

_____

_____

What are the four consistent factors in the life of the victim?

_____

_____

_____

_____

_____

_____

7

Four Degrees of Action

One question that I've received over the years is, "Exactly how *much* action is necessary to create success?" Not surprisingly, everyone is looking for the secret shortcut—and equally unsurprising is the following fact: There are no shortcuts. The more action you take, the better your chances are of getting a break. Disciplined, consistent, and persistent actions are more of a determining factor in the creation of success than any other combination of things. Understanding how to calculate and then take the right amount of action is more important than your concept, idea, invention, or business plan.

Most people fail only because they are operating at the wrong degree of action. To simplify action, we are going to break down your choices into four simple categories or degrees of action. Your four choices are:

1. Do nothing.
2. Retreat.
3. Take normal levels of action.
4. Take massive action.

Before I get into describing each of these, it is important to understand that everyone utilizes all four degrees of action at some time in their lives and especially in response to different areas of life. For instance, you might use massive action in your career but then completely retreat when it comes to your civic duties and responsibilities. Another person might do nothing when it comes to learning about social media, even retreat from it. Another might only take normal levels of action when it comes to eating healthy and exercising but then overexcel (take massive action) when it comes to destructive habits. A person is obviously going to excel and do best in those areas in which he or she invests the most attention and takes the most action.

Unfortunately, most people on the planet spend their time in the first through third degrees: doing nothing, retreating completely, or just operating at normal levels of activity. The first two degrees of action (do nothing and retreat) are the basis for failure, and the third degree (normal levels) will only create a normal existence at best. Only the most successful people hit on very high levels of action that I refer to as massive. So let's take a look at each of the four degrees to see what they mean and why you might choose each in a range of situations and areas of life.

The First Degree of Action

"Doing nothing" is exactly what it sounds like: no longer taking actions to move yourself forward in order to learn, achieve, or control some area. People who do nothing in their career, relationships, or whatever they want have probably given up on their dreams and are now willing to accept pretty much whatever comes their way. Despite how it may sound, do not assume that doing nothing requires no energy, effort, and work! *Regardless of which degree of action you operate in, they all require work in their own ways.* Signs that you are doing nothing include exhibiting boredom, lethargy, complacency, and lack of purpose. People in this group will find themselves spending their time and energy justifying their situations—which requires as much work as the other actions.

When the alarm goes off in the morning, the "do-nothing" group will not respond at all. Although it may appear that they're not taking action, it actually takes a lot of energy *not* to get up in the morning. It takes work to lose a job because of lack of production. It is work to be overlooked for a promotion and have to wait another year to be considered and then go home and explain it to your spouse. It takes tremendous effort to exist on this planet as an underappreciated and underpaid employee—and even more energy to make sense of it. The person not taking action has to make excuses for his or her condition; this requires tremendous creativity and effort. Salespeople who do nothing and then lose the sale more often than they win the sale have to explain to themselves, their spouses, and their bosses why they are not hitting their quotas. It's also interesting to note that those who do nothing in one area of their lives will find something they love to do and spend time doing those things—something for which they'll often take massive action. It could be online poker, gaming, biking, watching movies, reading books. Whatever it may be, I assure you that some area of life receives their full energy and attention. Those who do nothing will insist to their friends and family that they are happy and content and that all is right with them, which only serves to confuse everyone because it is evident that they are not living up to their full potential.

The Second Degree of Action

"Retreaters" are those who take actions in reverse—probably in order to avoid negative experiences that they imagine will come as a result of taking action. The retreater personifies the "fear-of-success" phenomenon. He or she has experienced results that were not fruitful (or that he or she did not perceive as fruitful) and has therefore decided to avoid taking further actions that might prompt this to occur again. Like the "do-nothings," retreaters justify their responses and believe it is in their best interest to remain operating at their current level. Retreaters claim to be doing so in order to avoid more rejection and/or failures; it is almost never the *actual* rejection or failure that has impacted them. More often than not, it's their impression and evaluation of what failing and rejection mean that is causing them to retreat.

Like doing nothing, retreating is an action that requires effort and hard work. Watch any healthy child, and you will see that it is not normal human behavior to retreat but rather to advance and conquer. Usually retreating only comes about as a result of being told to do so over and over. So many of us are instructed during childhood, "don't touch that," "be careful," "don't talk to him," "get away from that," and so on and then start to adopt retreat as an action. We tend to be pulled away from the very things about which we're most curious. Although it's often for our own good and supposedly keeps us safe, it can be difficult to rebound from these years of "holding back"—which might be why it's so difficult for so many of us to try new things later in life. We might even be encouraged to retreat by a work associate, friend, or family member who believes we are "too ambitious" or focused on a single area of our lives.

Regardless of the reasons why retreaters move themselves in the opposite direction of goals, the outcome is usually the same. I would imagine that everyone reading this knows someone who retreats, and perhaps you can even see how you retreat in some area of your life. Any realm in which you have assumed you can no longer advance and improve—and are now deciding that there is "nothing you can do"—would be considered an area of retreat. "The stock market sucks; I'm never investing in it again"—retreat. "Most marriages fail; I'm staying single"—retreat. "The acting business is too tough; I'll just be a waiter for the rest of my life"—retreat. "The job market is terrible; no one is hiring—I am filing for unemployment"—retreat. "I can't control the outcome of the election, so I'm not even going to bother to vote"—retreat! And notice the one thing that each of these scenarios has in common: They all still require some kind of action to be taken, even if it is just making a decision.

Those who retreat will spend a lot of time justifying *why* they are retreating. There is usually no arguing with these individuals, as they have typically convinced themselves completely that they're merely doing what they need to survive. They will then spend as much energy justifying their decision to retreat as the most successful person will in creating success. The best thing you can do for retreaters is to give them this book and allow them to identify for themselves that they are retreating. Once a person sees the four degrees of action and realizes that each requires energy, he or she may start to make other, healthier choices. After all, if you're going to expend effort, why not do so in the direction of success?

The Third Degree of Action

People who take normal levels of action are probably the most prevalent in our society today. This is the group that appears on the surface to be taking the necessary amounts of action and to be "normal." This level of action creates the middle class and is actually the most dangerous—because it's considered acceptable. People in this group spend their lives taking enough action to appear average and create normal lives, marriages, and careers; however, they never do quite enough to create real success. Unfortunately, a majority of the workforce takes normal degrees of action; it's those managers, executives, and companies that blend in more than they stand out. Although some members of this group may occasionally attempt to generate exceptional quality, they almost never create anything in exceptional quantities. The goal here is average—average marriages, health, careers, and finances. As long as average works, they are fine with it. They don't cause problems for others or themselves as long as conditions remain steady and predictable.

However, the moment market conditions become negatively impacted—and therefore less than normal—these people will suddenly realize that they're at risk. Add any serious change to the conditions in which people take only "normal" actions—which is certain to happen at some point— and all bets are off. It's not uncommon to encounter a situation that will challenge a person's life, career, marriage, business, or finances. When you have been taking only normal actions, you are even more susceptible to challenges that are certain to come your way. Any set of ordinary events, financial conditions, or stressful experiences can throw off a lifetime of typically "acceptable" levels of action and result in a serious degree of stress, uncertainty, and hurt.

Average, by definition, assumes "less than extraordinary." It is truly—to some degree or another—just an alternative description of retreat and no action. And it does even take into consideration the negative spiritual effects of a person knowing his or her true potential for action and then operating well below that which he or she is capable. Someone who takes average actions but is capable of much more is really electing to do some variation of doing nothing or retreating.

Be honest with yourself: Do you have more energy and creativity available than you're using? Average student, average marriage, average kids, average finances, average business, average products, average body type. . . . Who really desires "average"? Imagine that the products and services we're so often tempted to buy used "average" in their advertising: "This fairly average product can be found at an average price and delivers mediocre results." Who would buy such a product? People certainly don't go out of their way to find and pay for run-of-the-mill merchandise. "We are offering cooking classes that will guarantee that you become an average cook." I can do that now without taking classes. "New movie opening this weekend—average director, average acting, and the critics are raving, 'two hours of average action.'" Oh—can't wait to stand in line for that one!

Taking normal action is the most dangerous of the levels, because it is the most accepted by society. This level of action is authorized by the masses, and therefore people who don't take normal actions don't draw the necessary attention required to catapult them to success. Companies call me constantly to help the lower performers in their organization, yet they're overlooking the average and even top performers who are still only taking average actions. This book is probably more likely to wake up a "normal" action taker than someone who does nothing or retreats since the "do-nothing" person wouldn't even bother to buy this book in the first place and the retreater probably won't even go into the bookstore. People who take average or normal levels of action *will* buy the book—and hopefully come out from under the spell that has been placed on them. It is only by moving from the third to the fourth degree of action that a person can turn an average existence into an exceptional life.

The Fourth Degree: Massive Action

Though it might sound far-fetched, massive action is the most natural state of action there is for all of us. Look at children; they're in constant action, except when something is wrong. This was certainly true about me for the first 10 years my life.

It was nonstop massive action except when I was sleeping. Like most kids, I was full-out, all the time—with people frowning and hinting that maybe I should bring it down a notch or two. Did that happen to you? And have you done it to your own children?

Until adults started telling me otherwise, I didn't know anything else other than massive action. Even the most basic elements of the universe in which we live support massive amounts of action. Dive beneath the surface of the ocean and you will see constant and massive amounts of activity taking place. Just beneath the crust of the planet on which you walk is tremendous movement that never stops. Look inside an ant mound or into a beehive, and you will see colonies of living beings generating massive amounts of action in order to ensure their survival into the future. Nowhere in any of these environments are there signs of retreat or no activity or anything close to what would be considered normal levels.

My dad was a very hard worker and very much a strong disciplinarian who was definitely willing to take massive action. Unfortunately, he died when I was 10, which really hammered me. I look back now and realize that this event caused me to immediately begin retreating from areas of life in which I needed to take action. Meanwhile, I was expending *a lot* of energy in areas that really shouldn't have received any of my attention: drugs, alcohol, and a whole list of other useless activities. This continued throughout high school and then college, with a few more losses along the way. I continued to progressively retreat from those things that were good for me and continued concentrating on more destructive areas. I wasn't necessarily lazy or unmotivated; I simply didn't have the proper direction and was being misinformed about how to attack life.

I spent most of this time bored, without purpose, and gravitating to areas in life in which I could expend a lot of energy but not produce constructive results. I think this is something that most people endure at some time in their lives; I just happened to encounter it early on.

As I mentioned in a previous chapter, I experienced a major wakeup call at the age of 25. I knew that I had to get redirected or else I would pay the ultimate price. I made a decision to make the same commitment to the creation of success. Since it was already hard work *not* succeeding, I just changed the focus. Despite the fact that my father had been gone for 15 years, he still provided a great role model for me. He believed in a strong work ethic, was willing to do whatever it took to provide for his family, and went after success as though it was truly his duty and calling. I am sure he enjoyed the financial rewards and sense of personal accomplishment that came with his achievements; however, it was also clear to me that he thought it to be his responsibility to his family, church, name, and even God. He just ran out of time!

Once I finally woke up from my period of misdirection and misinformation, I committed all my energy to my career. Ever since the age of 25, the one thing I did right—whether it was in my first sales job or the first company I built—was to approach whatever task was before me with massive amounts of action. It was never retreat, no action, or even average amounts; it was constant, persistent, and immense attack on the target.

Massive action is actually the level of action that creates new problems—and until you create problems, you're not truly operating at the fourth stage of action. When I started my seminar business at the age of 29, I employed the 10X Rule to create a name for myself. I would start my day at 7 AM and not get back to my hotel until 9 PM. I spent the day cold calling companies and offering to do presentations to their sales and management teams. I would visit as many as 40 organizations in a single day. I remember being in El Paso, Texas—a city where I had never been, knew no one, and no one knew me. Within two weeks, I had seen every business in that market. Although I was unsuccessful in making every one of them a client, I certainly secured more business by taking massive action than I would have otherwise.

A real estate agent once traveled with me to observe firsthand how I was growing my business. After three days of shadowing me, he admitted, "There is no way I can do this for another day. I am only *riding* with you, and I'm exhausted." I approached every day like my life depended on the actions I took. I refused to leave the city without knowing I did everything possible to meet every business owner there. Cold "visiting" companies taught me more about taking massive action than any other activity I have ever done and has proved more valuable to me in my other ventures.

When you are taking massive action, you aren't thinking in terms of how many hours you work. When you start operating at the fourth degree of action, your mind-set will shift and so will your results. You will end up instigating opportunities that you will have to address earlier, later, and in a different way than you would on a "normal" day, so a routine day will become a thing of the past. I continued this commitment to massive action until one day it was no longer an unusual activity but a habit for me. It was interesting to see how many people would ask me, "Why are you still out this late at night?" "What are you doing calling on us on a Saturday?" "You never quit, do you?" "I wish my people worked like this." And even— "What are you *on*?" I was on something; I was treating success as my duty, obligation, and responsibility, and massive action was my ace in the hole. Signals that you're taking massive action are having people comment upon and admire your level of activity.

However, you can't think in terms of compliments or how many hours you work or even how much money you're making when you're operating at this degree. Instead, you have to approach each day as though your life and your future depend on your ability to take massive action. When I started my first business, I *had* to make it work; there was simply no two ways about it! If I wanted people to know about me and about what I represented, then I was going to have to *do* a lot—period. The problem wasn't competition; it was obscurity. No one even knew who I was. This has been the single biggest problem I've encountered in every business I have built, and I imagine that it's one most entrepreneurs face. People don't know you or about your new product—and the only way to burst through obscurity is by taking massive action. I didn't have money to invest in advertising, so I spent all my energy on phone calls, traditional mail, e-mail, cold calls, return calls, visits, and more calls. This level of massive action may sound—and is indeed exhausting at times. However, it will create more certainty and security for you than probably any other education or training you will ever receive.

I have been called a lot of things due to my commitment to action—a workaholic, obsessive, greedy, never satisfied, driven, and even manic. Yet every time I have been labeled, it's always been by someone operating at less than the fourth degree of action. I have never had someone who is more successful than I am considering my excessive action to be a bad thing—because successful people know firsthand what it takes to achieve this kind of success. They know themselves how to get where they want to go and would never identify massive action as undesirable in any way.

Taking massive action means making somewhat unreasonable choices and then following these up with even more action. This level of action will be considered by some to be borderline insane, well beyond the agreed-upon social norm— and will always create new problems. But remember: If you don't create new problems, then you're not taking enough action.

You can also expect to be criticized and labeled by others when you start taking massive action. The second you start hitting it big, you will immediately be judged by the mediocre. People who operate at the other three levels of action will be threatened by your activity level and will often make it seem somehow "wrong" in order to make themselves right. These people cannot stand seeing others succeed at these levels and will do everything to stop them. Whereas a sane person would step up to your level, a mediocre person will tell you that you are wasting your time, this won't work in your industry, it is a turnoff to your clientele, no one will want to work with you, and so on. Even management occasionally discourages employees from putting forth this kind of substantial effort. You will know you are stepping into the realm of massive action when you (1) create new problems for yourself and (2) start to receive criticism and warning from others. But stay strong. This activity will break you out of the hypnotic state of mediocrity that you've been taught to accept.

And in order to deliver at that level of massive action, you must take every opportunity that comes your way. For example, my wife is an actress. I tell her all the time to say yes to every audition, regardless of whether she is prepared or whether she thinks the part is right for her. It's better to suck and be seen than not to be seen at all! "But what if I bomb?" my wife asks me. I tell her, "Hollywood is filled with terrible actors that are still somehow working." Maybe they won't pick you for the part you went up for but will see that you're perfect for some other part. The goal is to be seen, thought of, and considered—in one way or another. Your only problem is obscurity, not talent. In order for the endeavor you've chosen to work out for you, you have to make constant, relentless effort. Massive action can never hurt you and will always help you. This is also one place where quantity is more important than quality. Money and power follow attention, so whoever can get the most attention is the person who takes the most action and sooner or later will get the most results.

No one is going to come to your house and make your dreams come true. No one is going to march into your company and make your products known to the world. In order to stand out from the crowd—and for customers to even consider your products, services, and organization—you must take massive action. I talked about the importance of domination in my last book, *If You're Not First, You're Last*. I was not alluding to physical domination but rather to mentally occupying the space of the public—so that when people think of your product, service, or industry, they think of *you*. Making massive action a discipline will break you through obscurity, increase your value to the marketplace, and help you generate success in any area you elect.

Exercise

When was a time in your life when you were taking massive action and winning?

_____

_____

_____

_____

What will you immediately create when you take massive action?

_____

_____

_____

_____

What can you expect those who don't take massive action to say to those who do?

_____

_____

_____

_____

What other things may happen as you start to take massive action?

_____

_____

_____

_____

8

Average Is a Failing Formula

Look around, and chances are you'll see a world filled with average. Although this is—as I have previously stated—the "acceptable" level of activity upon which the middle class is built, there is a growing amount of evidence that this thinking is unworkable. Jobs are being shipped overseas, and unemployment is becoming even more rampant. Members of the middle class are unable to get their heads above water, people are living longer than their savings, and entire companies and industries are being wiped out as a result of average products, average management, average workers, average actions, and average thinking.

This "addiction to average" can kill the possibility of making your dreams a reality. Consider the following statistics: The average worker reads an average of less than one book a year and works an average of 37.5 hours per week. This same person makes 319 times less money than the top U.S. CEOs, who claim to read more than 60 books a year. Many of these financially successful executives are maligned for the huge sums of money they receive; however, we often fail to appreciate what these people have done to get where they are today. Although it might not always look like they're working very hard, we often dismiss the fact that they somehow managed to attend the right schools, make the right connections, and then did what was necessary to move up the food chain. It all required substantial action on their part. You can resent them if you choose, but that doesn't change the fact that they are being rewarded for the success they've achieved.

After the economy suffered so greatly in 2008, Starbucks founder Howard Schultz began to do what almost every other CEO in America was doing—cutting expenses and getting rid of nonperforming locations. He then did something that most CEOs did *not* do: he traveled all over the country to meet with Starbucks patrons. Long after the average worker had gone home, billionaire Schultz was visiting his stores and meeting with coffee drinkers to find out how Starbucks could better satisfy customers. Although the media didn't do much reporting on this, it was a pretty astounding pattern of events. Here was a guy making his way across the country at 9 PM to get feedback from people buying his products. This is a prime example of embracing a "greater-than-average" thought and action process. This is clearly above and beyond what the marketplace—and any customer—expects. It far exceeded any action considered commonplace for a CEO, and Starbucks' very solid and strong growth was reflected in stock charts.

This company makes a product that people do not absolutely *need*—especially during troubling economic times. Yet Starbucks continues to sell and grow both its brand and return to investors. This demonstrates that although the quality of the product is clearly important, the individuals who work for an organization are truly the force that will make the most difference. Schultz knew exactly how to approach the situation.

Despite the recession, despite temporary contraction, he still managed to "expand" his organization—not necessarily with more locations but by using his personal energy, resources, and creativity to take massive action, touch each of his stores and many of his patrons, and increase the presence of his brand and its revenues.

Any undertaking that includes accepting average will fail you sooner or later. Anything conducted in standard amounts simply won't get the job done. The normal levels of action at which most people operate fail to take into account the effects of various forces—such as gravity, age, resistance, timing, and the unexpected. When average actions hit any resistance, competition, loss or lack of interest, negative or challenging market conditions, or all of these, you will find your project tumbling down.

Finally, I want you to take into consideration the concerted efforts of individuals and groups who actually impede your efforts. Although I am not one to be paranoid or live in fear, I learned the very expensive lesson that these people do exist when I was approached by a group who claimed to want to make me their partner. However, they never intended to bring me in as a partner but instead intended from the outset to steal from me the success I had created in my life. I never planned on this in any of my equations, and it literally robbed me of years of efforts. So take it from me—you cannot plan on everything, and people will try to take from you what they are unable to create themselves.

When I look back and attempt to analyze what happened with these criminals, I realize that I was susceptible to their enticement because I was no longer operating at 10X levels. This really opened my eyes to the fact that the moment I started resting on my laurels—and thought that I could "coast a bit"—I made myself a target. It is almost impossible to plan for every situation. In your lifetime, you will experience extraordinary conditions, some of which may be hostile and unpleasant. The best way to plan is to condition your thinking and your actions to 10X levels. Succeed so big that no one person or event or series of missteps can take you down! Average levels of anything will fail you—or at the very least, put you at risk! If, on the other hand, you create more success than you want or need, you'll always be prepared—even when those who can't create success for themselves try to steal it from you.

Although I experienced years of success at levels that others deemed to be quite impressive, I knew in my heart that I had quit taking massive action. And sure enough, these guys decided to peel a little of my success away from me—and got away with it. It was quite an expensive and humbling setback—but it really woke me up to the fact that you are never safe to move to normal levels of involvement and activity. Once you do so, I assure you, what you have and what you dreamed of will start to disappear. This holds true for your health, marriage, wealth, and spiritual condition. Normal gets you just that—normal.

See what average thoughts and actions will get you—average problems that can quickly become overwhelming problems. What if you live 20 years longer than your savings? Many of us will have to take care of other family members because they didn't have a 10X mind-set or operate at 10X levels. What about the possibility of long-term health issues or some state of economic emergency that hasn't been foreseen? What happens to entire classes of people who made average financial plans when faced with extended periods of very difficult economic times or decades of extended unemployment? Average is a failing plan!

Average doesn't work in *any* area of life. Anything that you give only average amounts of attention to will start to subside and will eventually cease to exist. Companies, industries, artists, products, and individuals who continue into the future successfully are those who approach every activity with the outlook that average is just not good enough. You need to change your commitment and thinking to be far above any concepts of average. I promise that when you do so, you will immediately start influencing other areas of your life. Your friends and family will start to change, results will improve, you will find yourself getting luckier, you may experience time flying by, and the actions you are taking will begin to improve your associations with people.

Average is also the reason why most new companies fail. A couple of people get together, have a great idea, write a business plan, start a company, and base their predictions on everything going in their favor. They may even create what they consider to be conservative projections. "Let's say we show the product to 10 people. We're bound to sell at least three of them. That's conservative and realistic." Someone in the group says, "Let's cut that in half to be especially safe. Can we still make it?" They decide that even based on the more conservative plan, they will be successful. But they didn't correctly assess how many people they would have to call on just to *do* the initial 10 presentations. Even the most amazing product on earth might require 100 calls just to get the 10 meetings. Just because you have the next step of the project completely planned out doesn't mean that the rest of the world is there with you. They've committed to their schedules, their products, and their projects. Merely getting the opportunity to see the right people will take enormous effort and persistence. Most people are building business plans based on average considerations and ways of thinking, not the massive amounts of action that are necessary to push through.

When new ideas come together, they are influenced by the excitement and enthusiasm of those who generate them. Many negative considerations—such as competition, the economy, market conditions, manufacturing, lending, raising money, the preoccupation of your clients with other projects, and the like—are set at what everyone considers normal or average difficulty. Then, when optimistic projections prove unrealistic, even the most conservative objectives are missed. A key partner might get sick, there might be some significant change in economic conditions, or some global event might occur that shifts everyone's attention for the next six months. People involved in the new venture start to lose their enthusiasm, bickering ensues, and as things become more difficult than was originally considered, failure emerges as a likely possibility. The partners go through more money than anyone projected—and with no income. One of the dreamers begins to have second thoughts and wonders if perhaps he should bail since the players don't seem mentally, emotionally, or physically prepared to take the massive action necessary to push through market resistance.

Continuing with this scenario, in order to resolve the lack of income problems, members of the group try to borrow or raise money from their friends—where they hit even more resistance. They realize that it will become increasingly difficult for most people to ante up to the "unreasonable" amounts of relentless 10X actions that are necessary to see things through and were missing from the business plan. The partners start to believe that their company relies more intensely on raising money than it does on increasing actions because they didn't correctly estimate the 10X level of thoughts and actions necessary to keep going.

Average assumes—incorrectly, of course—that everything operates stably. People optimistically overestimate how well things will go and then underestimate how much energy and effort it will take just to push things through. Anyone who has made it in business will support this concept. You simply cannot train or prepare for normal amounts of gravity or resistance, competition, and market conditions. Don't think average; think massive. Compare your actions to having to carry a 1,000-pound backpack that you will wear every day into a 40-miles-per-hour wind on a 20-degree upward slope. Prepare for massive, persistent action, and you will win!

Most businesses fail because they are unable to sell their ideas, products, and services at prices high enough to sustain the company and fund its activities. The company isn't able to collect revenue in quantities great enough because the people with whom the company has been built—employees, customers, and vendors—also take only average amounts of action.

Average never yields anything more than average and usually much less. Average thinking and actions will only guarantee you misery, uncertainty, and failure. Rid yourself of everything that is average including the advice you get and friends you keep. Sound too tough? Remember that success is your duty, obligation, and responsibility. And since there is no shortage of success, any apparent limitations you are experiencing might simply be the result of thinking and acting average. Rid yourself of every concept of average. Study what average people do, and prohibit yourself and your team from considering average as an option. Surround yourself with exceptional thinkers and doers. Let your friends, family, and work associates know that you treat average like a terminal disease. Remember, average anything will never get you to an extraordinary life. Look up the word average and see for yourself what it holds for you—typical, ordinary, common. That should be enough to abandon the concept from all your considerations.

Exercise

Write down the names of people who you know operate at only average levels.

_____
_____
_____
_____
_____

Write down three times in your life when average actions caused you to come up short.

_____
_____
_____
_____
_____

Write down the names of people who you know are exceptional and describe how they are different from average.

_____
_____
_____
_____
_____

Look up the definition of average (as an adjective) and write it here.

_____
_____
_____
_____
_____

9

10X Goals

I believe that one of the major reasons why people don't stick to their goals and fail to accomplish them is because they fail to set them high enough from the beginning. I have read many books on goal setting and have even been to seminars on this topic, and I constantly see people set goals and then either never get started or bail on them. Frequently and regularly, most of us have been warned against setting goals "too high." The reality is that if you start small, you are probably going to go small. People's failure to think big enough usually means they will never *act* big enough, often enough, or persistently enough! After all, who gets excited about so-called realistic goals? And who can stay excited about anything with an—at best—average payoff? This is why people begin to bail on projects when they experience any kind of resistance; their goals are not big enough. To maintain your enthusiasm, you have to make your goals substantial enough that they keep your attention. Average and realistic goals are almost always a letdown to the person setting them—who is then unable to fuel his or her goals with the actions necessary.

Indeed, most people are so apathetic about their goals that they only write them down once a year. As far as I'm concerned, nothing worth doing is done only once or twice a year. The things upon which your life depends most are based on the actions you take daily. That is why I make sure to always do two things: (1) I write my goals down every day and (2) I choose objectives that are just out of reach. This opens me up to my full potential, which I use to fuel my action each day. Some people suggest that setting improbable goals might cause a person to become disappointed and lose interest. But if your goals are so small that you don't even need to consider them on a daily basis, then you are going to lose interest!

A good idea is to word your goals as though you've already accomplished them. I keep a legal pad next to my bed so that I can record my goals first thing each morning and right before I go to bed at night. I also keep one in my office on which I record new and improved objectives. The following are examples of some of the goals I am currently working on and how I write them down. Notice that I word them as though I have already achieved each of them (when I have yet to do so).

I own 5,000+ apartments that return over 12 percent positive cash flow.

I am in perfect health and physical condition.

My net worth is over $100 million.

My income is over $1 million a month.

I have written and published 12 or more best-selling books.

My marriage is alive and healthy and a positive model for others.

I am more in love with my wife every day.

I have two beautiful and healthy children.

I have no debt except that which is paid by others.

I own a beautiful home on the ocean that has no debt.

I own a ranch in Colorado that has incredible views of the mountains and horses and is my ideal scene.

I own companies that I am able to control from a distance and have great people working with me.

My children are friends with the most powerful people on the planet.

I am making a positive difference in my community and politics.

I continue to create unique programs that people want and that improve the quality of others lives.

I have endless energy and interest in my career.

I have a hit TV show that has been on for five seasons.

I am one of the largest donors to my church.

Keep in mind that these are some of my goals and are only being used to give you an example of how I word them. Also note that they are things that are yet to be achieved, not things that have been achieved.

Average goal setting cannot and will not fuel massive 10X actions. If you approach an endeavor with average thinking, you will start to give up the moment you come up against any challenges, resistance, or less than optimal conditions—unless you have some big juicy purpose as your engine. To get through resistance, you must have a big reason to get there. The bigger and more *un*realistic your goals are—and the more they're aligned to your purpose and duty—the more they'll energize and fuel your actions.

For example, let's say I want to save $100 million in a bank account. Does anyone need $100 million? No! It is a goal—and the bigger and juicier it is, the more likely you will be motivated to move in that direction and through resistance. If you want to add even more energy to your goals, then make sure they are tied to something even bigger. For instance, someone who wants to earn money but doesn't have a constructive goal for what to do with it may only produce the money and then just waste it. When you are setting a goal, be sure you are clear about what you want it for, and then tie it to a greater purpose. Think massive and broad when setting your goals. Many people make money a target and set a goal to save it but then just destroy the wealth that was created. Look at how many people just wanted to get rich, did so, and then died broke. So having goals aligned with other goals will start to actually help you. Let's say one of my goals is to save $100 million and another goal is to use that money to help my church and fund programs to improve conditions for mankind. This is an example of combining goals that will generate the fuel and horsepower to drive my actions and all my goals.

One of the first jobs I ever had was at McDonald's. I hated it—and not because it was McDonald's. I hated it because it was not lined up with my goals and purposes. The guy who worked next to me loved his job because it aligned with his goals and purposes. I was the guy making $7 an hour because I wanted some spending money, and he was the guy making $7 an hour but who wanted to learn the business and open 100 franchises. He didn't understand why I wasn't excited, and I didn't understand why he *was*. I was fired, and he went on to own franchises. Your goals are there to fuel the actions you will need to take—so make them big and make them often and then tie them in with your other greater purposes.

Ask yourself whether the goals you have set are equal to your potential. Most people will admit that their goals are well below their potential—because most of the world has been convinced, persuaded, and even educated to set small, attainable, and realistic goals. If you're a parent, I am sure you have heard yourself suggest this to your children—or maybe you heard it from your own parents or in your work environment.

Never set realistic goals; you can get a realistic life without setting goals for it.

I truly despise the word "realistic" because it is based on what others—who have probably been operating at only the first three degrees of action—have accomplished and believe possible. Realistic thinking is based on what others think is possible—but they are not you and have no way of knowing your potential and purposes. If you are going to set goals based on what others think, then be sure you do it based on what the giants on this planet think. They will be the first to tell you, "Don't base your goals on what I have done because you can do even more." But what if you set goals based on those of the top players in the world? Steve Jobs's goal, for instance, is to "ding" the universe—to create products that forever change our planet. Look at what he has done with Apple and Pixar. If you are going to set goals comparable to those of others, then at the very least pick the giants who have already created massive success.

Many people find themselves on the path they're on simply because they're doing what other—average—people have done. Most people go to college not because they want to but because they are told to go. Most people belong to the religion they belong to only because they were brought up that way. Most people speak only the language that their family speaks and never take the time to learn another language. Most of us are influenced by the decisions our parents, teachers, and friends have made and then the limitations set by them and for us. I bet that if I asked your five closest associates about their goals, I'd probably be able to identify some of yours as well. You—and your goals—are manipulated by your surroundings.

I will never tell another person what his or her goals should be. However, I would advise that when you do set your goals, take into account that you have been educated with restrictions. Be aware of this so that you don't underestimate the possibilities. Then take the following into account: (1) You are setting these for *you*—not for anyone else. (2) Anything is possible. (3) You have much more potential than you realize. (4) Success is your duty, obligation, and responsibility. (5) There is no shortage of success. (6) Regardless of the size of the goal, it will require work. Once you've reviewed these concepts, then sit down and write out your goals. And then be willing to rewrite them every day until they are achieved.

If you underestimate your potential, then it is impossible to set appropriately sized targets. Set the goals too small, and you will not gear up for the massive action necessary. I know the concept of *The 10X Rule* is NOT for everyone. It is clearly not for anyone who is willing to accept average or mediocrity or for those who prefer to kick back and settle for the left-overs. It is not for those who want to depend on hope and prayer for their success. The 10X Rule is meant for the few people obsessed with creating an exceptional life—and who want to be in charge of that process. The 10X Rule removes the concepts of luck and chance from your business equation and shows you exactly what mind-set you must embrace in order to lock in massive success.

Consider the following scenario: Let's say that you are setting your financial goals. In 2009, the president of the United States said that people who make $250,000 should be considered rich. Keeping with the current trend, your tax bill will be at least $100,000, leaving you with a remaining $150,000. After you make payments on two cars, make a mortgage payment, pay your property taxes, and feed, clothe, and school your kids, you might have $20,000 left. If you save that money for the next 20 years, you'll end up with around $400,000—assuming nothing goes wrong. Now take into account the fact that your parents—possibly both your parents and your in-laws—didn't plan for their own retirement properly. They are going to outlive their savings by about 15 years and will depend on you to take care of them. If any of this happens, you will find out quite quickly, and too late, that you underestimated your financial goals and will spend more effort just trying to manage what you have created than what it took to accumulate it. And remember, in addition to taking care of your parents, you have to fund your own retirement years. Additionally, this scenario assumes no increases in the cost of living, no bad news, no emergencies, and no major events. Throw in just a little of what has happened in the last couple of years, and you will see that 90 percent of the population has underestimated the goals and targets necessary to fund their lifestyles, much less their life's purposes. "Small" thinking has and always will be punished in one way or another.

We live on a planet where the primary belief is an underestimation of everything. The best business schools in the country cite undercapitalization as one of the top reasons for companies' failures. This is caused by a miscalculation of how much cash a company would burn through before its product caught on—and is yet another example of how average doesn't cut it.

The biggest regret of my life is not the fact that I haven't worked my ass off—because I have. It's that I didn't set targets 10 times higher than what I originally thought I could accomplish from the very beginning. Why? Because my goals were influenced and limited greatly by the way I was brought up. I am not blaming anyone; it is just a fact. I spent the first 30 years of my business career getting the 10X effort part right and will spend the next 25 years getting the 10X goal-setting part right. So I recommend you do the following:

1. Set 10X targets.
2. Align them with your other purposes.
3. Write them down every day—when you wake up and before you go to sleep.

Exercise

Write down how your upbringing has influenced your goal setting.

_____
_____
_____
_____
_____

What are some goals you would set if you knew you could achieve them?

_____
_____
_____
_____
_____

What are other goals/purposes that align with primary goals that would further fuel your actions?

_____
_____
_____
_____
_____

Look at the list of goals I wrote and find two things they all have in common.

_____
_____
_____
_____
_____

CHAPTER

10

Competition Is for Sissies

One of the great lies perpetuated by mankind is the idea that competition is good. Good for whom—exactly? It might help provide customers with choices and compel others to do better. However, in the business world, you always want to be in a position to *dominate*—not compete. If the old saying is, "Competition is healthy," the new saying is, "If competition is healthy, then domination is immunity!"

From what I have seen, competing with others limits a person's ability to think creatively because he or she is constantly watching what someone else is doing. The reason my first business has been so successful is because I created sales programs that introduced a truly original way of selling for which there was no competition. It was clearly a new way to think and approach selling. No one had done anything other than just copy one another for the past 200 years. So I ignored the competition and did something created a new sales process called "Information-Assisted Selling." This was before the Internet and before consumers had information readily available to them. I predicted that sellers would have to throw away the old ways of selling and learn how to use information to assist them. Although I was ahead of my time and traditional thinkers resisted once the Internet hit critical mass, information-assisted selling became a way of selling, and my competition was left holding on to antiquated systems and processes. And I came out on top, because people were thrilled to see something completely new. Forward thinkers don't copy. They don't compete—they create. They also don't look at what others have done.

Never make it your goal to *compete*. Instead, do everything you can to dominate your sector in order to avoid spending your time chasing someone else. Don't let another company set the pace; make this *your* organization's job. Stay ahead of the pack. Make it so that they want to chase *you* and try to be like you, not the other way around. This doesn't mean that you shouldn't study others' best practices in industry trends; however, you want to make it your job to take those concepts to another level. For example, Apple makes computers and smartphones; it didn't simply copy what Dell, IBM, Rimm, and others were doing. Apple doesn't compete; it dominates, it sets the pace, and it lets others try to duplicate its success. Don't set your goals at a competitive level. Set them at a level that will overshadow and dominate your sector completely.

How do you dominate, you may wonder? The first step is to decide to dominate. Then the best way to dominate is to do what others refuse to do. That's right—do what they will *not* do. This will allow you to immediately carve out a space for yourself and develop an unfair advantage. Let me be clear: I want an *unfair* advantage if I can create one. Though I am always ethical, I never play fair. I seek out ways in which I can get an unfair advantage—and one surefire way to do this is to do what others won't. Find something they cannot do, maybe because of their size or their commitment to other projects, and then exploit that. Maybe they are cutting back during a time when the economy is uncertain. This would be your moment to expand into those spaces where they are contracting. A company I was working with that was in dental implants told me the leader in the field had cut all travel expenses and elected that all client contact is done by phone and over the Internet. To get a competitive advantage, we decided to dominate the personal contacts while the leader retreated. Domination—not competition!

Never play by the agreed-upon norms within which others operate. The rules, norms, and traditions of any group or industry are usually traps that prevent new ideas, higher levels of greatness, and domination. You don't want to just be in a race; you want to be at the top of the list of considerations. Even better, you would like to be the *only* one considered as a viable solution. You need to adopt the attitude that you have so much power in your space that your clients, your market, and even your competition automatically think about *you first* when they think about what you do. IBM did this so successfully that all PCs were referred to as IBMs. There was a time when Xerox accomplished this so successfully with copiers that you didn't talk about making copies but rather Xeroxing. That is pure domination of a sector and not correctly protecting your trademarked name. The goal at my sales training company is not to compete with others in the space for the revenue or the clients. Our goal is to literally make sure that every human being on planet earth equates Grant Cardone with sales training. Achievable? Probably not, but it is the target we use for making decisions. We aren't competing with anyone else to be the best in a sector. Our goal is to dominate the thinking of all people so that my name becomes synonymous with sales training. Google the term "sales motivation" and watch my video pop up. That is the way to approach a sector, goal, or any endeavor—to own it completely.

You can always learn from those who want to compete; just don't chase them. Sam Walton, founder of Wal-Mart, was said to shop other stores weekly in order to see what they were doing well and improve on that. At the same time, he also had the goal of domination, not competition. If you are going to duplicate the best of what others do, then hammer away at them, champion that practice, and make it yours. Hone their "specialties" until they become *your* advantage. Do so to the point where you become the expert and leader in that area and dominate it so incredibly that they no longer even want to attempt it. You don't have to be first to the space, but it is important to be considered first in the space—if you get what I mean. The message you want to send to the marketplace through your persistent actions is, "No one can keep up with me. I'm not going away. I am not a competitor. I am *the space*."

Most of you will have less money than some of the leaders in your space. Even if you have less money than other players in the market, that doesn't mean you're at a disadvantage. Although they may be able to outspend or outadvertise you, you can certainly outwork them by using social media, personal visits, mail, e-mail, networking, and so on. Create campaigns using the resources you do have. There is no shortage of energy, effort, creativity, or how much you can make contact with your clients. Use variations of campaigns of offers, information, video, links, third-party validation, mail, e-mails, phone calls, and personal visit combinations to counter the expensive and often wasteful ad campaigns used by the bigger players. *Warning*: When using activity to counter "deep pocket" advertising of competitors, *never* underestimate how much activity it takes to be noticed and to maintain attention in your space. For example, people think that they can post twice a day on Facebook or Twitter and that they are creating an effect. You don't understand massive action if you think in twos and you definitely are underestimating the size of the Internet if you think a couple of posts are going to get you noticed. Like every other aspect of growing your business, you have to keep showing up over and over and make it obvious that you are not going away.

The good thing about social media is anyone can play in the space, regardless of his or her financial situation. It allows for unlimited creativity, and rewards only those who use it consistently and persistently. When I first started playing with social media, I posted twice a day. I don't know what I was thinking—it was a moment of "little think." We simultaneously began sending out e-mail strategies once a month and found ourselves getting requests from people who wanted to be removed from our e-mail campaign. My colleagues suggested I back off. That is when I woke up and came to my senses. Instead of backing off, I made the order to increase the number of posts to 10 times what we had been doing. I then instructed my employees to start sending out electronic strategies twice a week instead of monthly (eight times) and began personally posting comments on Twitter 48 times a day (once every 30 minutes). Each of them was written by me, and they were set up to be dropped in at a certain time. Although you might assume that the complaints and "unsubscribe" requests would increase with this massive outflow campaign, they didn't. Instead, we started receiving e-mails and posts of admiration for my activity level, and compliments for my willingness to provide people with free sales and motivational information. The questions came flooding in: "How can you do all this? How big is your staff? Where do you find the time? Do you ever rest?" And for every person commenting, there had to be another 1,000 thinking something similar . . . and who do you think they were thinking about? This was not expensive to do and only cost me energy, effort, and creativity. At the same time I was doing this, the guy who most people compare me with was asked what he thought about social media. He responded, "I am still evaluating it." While he is evaluating, I am beating it to death. I posted one day on Twitter, "I am going to make Twitter my little bitch."

This is a great example of domination and outrageous think and action that doesn't cost money. Think about domination like this: You can't dominate if you don't penetrate, and you won't penetrate by using reasonable levels of activity. Your biggest problem is obscurity—other people don't know you and aren't thinking about you.

Another problem for all of us is just getting through the amount of noise in the marketplace. You have to do two things: (1) get noticed and (2) get through the noise. In my case, had we made a decision to back off in order to satisfy a few complainers, we would not have expanded our contact base. The more I posted, the more people liked us. The more we put out, the more people we helped. As we blasted on this new program, we even saw posts from competitors mocking me. Yet even these comments brought attention to me and my business. Two things will happen when you take the right amount of action: (1) You will get a new set of problems and (2) your competition will start promoting you. I love it when I have made such an impact that others who don't even know me are having conversations that raise awareness about my business, my products, and what I am up to.

Determine the capability, actions, and mind-set of those against whom you compete. Do what they will not do, go where they will not go, and think and take actions in 10X quantities that they cannot comprehend. Don't get too involved in competing on best practices; take your actions to a point considered unreasonable by the world, where you are doing those things that only you and your company would, could, or are willing to do—something I call "only practices."

For one company I once consulted with, we identified places in which "only practices" could be employed. We discovered that the industry in general struggled with the practice of following up with customers. So we looked at what our competitors would *not* do and found that none of them would call back clients as they left the store. This led the company to immediately initiate programs during which clients were called back as they drove out of the parking lot. Managers then immediately started calling clients' cell phones as they left the company's premises and asked them to return. If the call went to voicemail, the manager left a message requesting the client to, "Please come back immediately. I have something you must see." Or the manager would send a text suggesting that the company had something to show the client *right away*. If there was no successful contact made, another manager repeated the callback program that same day and again the next morning. The results were crazy. Almost 50 percent of the clients returned immediately, and almost 80 percent of those became buyers at that time. Another 20 percent returned as a result of the later calls and increased the sales of that organization to new levels. This is an example of "only practices."

It doesn't matter what you do—it does matter that your goal be to dominate your sector with actions, that are immediate, consistent, and persistent and at levels that no one else is willing to operate at or duplicate. Take any action, and take it to a level that will separate you and your company from everyone else who might be in your space. Be willing to spend every last bit of energy, effort, and creativity on distinguishing yourself as the only player there. Learn how to dominate by being first in the minds of your market, your clients, and even your competitors. Market conditions won't improve until you improve the way you think and approach the market. Even if you are in a weak market, you suffer less when you dominate it. Weak markets actually create opportunities because the players in those markets typically have become dependent and weak because they don't know how to operate in a more challenging environment. Don't feel sorry for them; dominate them. They're not having bad luck; their average think and actions are simply failing them. The marketplace is brutal and will punish anyone and everyone who does not take the right amounts of action. Now is the time to shift into making your every thought and action aimed at dominating your sector, market, competition—and the every thought of your potential clients. Quit thinking about competing. Despite what everyone says, it's not healthy. It's for sissies.

Exercise

What is the difference between dominating and competing?

_____

_____

_____

_____

_____

_____

_____

_____

If competition is healthy, domination is _____
_____.

What is the difference between best practices and only practices?

_____

_____

_____

_____

_____

_____

_____

What are some practices you can do that would separate you from your competition?

_____

_____

_____

_____

_____

_____

_____

CHAPTER

11

Breaking Out of the
Middle Class

Please don't take offense at what I write in this chapter.
I know many of you have spent your whole life trying
to get to the middle class, and I am about to tell you it is
the wrong goal. Have an open mind. I am going to write an
entire book on this topic one day—but for now, let's just think
about breaking out of what I call the "middle-class mentality."
I believe I can make the case that the middle class is the group
hurt most by its members' thinking and actions—leaving
themselves to be the most susceptible to insecurity and pain.
Although this is a group that many people aspire to be a part
of, it's also the group that seems the most trapped, manipulated, and at risk. Is the middle class really as good a status
as you've been made to believe? Do you even know what it
means to be middle class or what puts a person in this group?
Before you make a decision about where you are going or the

group you're striving to belong to, it would be wise to inspect the statistics of that group.

The Incomes of the Middle Class

Reports from Wikipedia and the 2008 Census suggest that the middle-class income range is somewhere between $35,000 to $50,000 per year. Read another set of studies, and these figures are between $22,000 and $65,000 per year. It's no secret that it would be extremely difficult to live on either of these income levels in an urban area like New York or LA—much less feel financially secure. This experience is not what most people would consider a desirable situation.

The middle class is further divided into the upper and lower middle class. The upper middle class usually consists of people who have substantial assets and household earnings of over $1 million per year, although there is nothing to substantiate what makes $1 million the mark. I guess it just sounds good. Most people consider $1 million to be a lot of money—until they have it. Then they realize that it doesn't go very far since a person's decisions and considerations tend to change once he or she enters a new income bracket.

The people in the supposed upper middle class occupy noticeably higher positions in their offices and are considered financially more stable than many of their peers. This may very well be the case—until any sort of economic destruction occurs. Then we tend to see that even this group is unprotected. Admittedly, members of this group should experience a considerable rise in their incomes due to the economic growth of the nation in good times. They have higher disposable incomes than many of their counterparts in the lower middle class, which consists of people who have basic educational qualifications and an annual income of between $30,000 and $60,000. The lower middle class constitutes a large part of our country's total population. This set frequently struggles to reach the upper middle class's level; however, when economic hardship takes hold, everyone gets pulled down.

A client of mine recently asked me via text message on the 26th of a recent month, "Grant, I have to net $10,000 to keep my doors open this month. How can I do this?" I happened to get his message during a Sunday football game, so I asked him, "Are you watching the game today?" He texted me back, "Yes." I then replied, "What are you doing taking a Sunday off to watch the game?! You should be out distributing fliers, spending every second of every hour trying to create income in excess of what you need. And by the way, you need $100,000 in net profits—not $10,000." "Sunday," he responded, "is a day of rest." Oh boy. I shot back, "It is for those that worked the other six days! The Lord wasn't talking to the people who are short on funds and haven't earned the day of rest. So turn off the game, get off your couch, and go get the money you need! Quit being a middle-class slave, and go create the income you need to secure wealth and financial freedom—for yourself and your household and your company!" I think he got the message.

My client is at risk because he has been operating based on what he needs and therefore is just "getting by." Unfortunately, this middle-class mentality will not create financial security. The banks dried up on him; he could no longer depend on credit for his cushion, and he can now depend only on his actions. This is the problem with many members of the middle class. They go after what they've deemed *necessary* rather than ever going really big. Most people believe that a comfortable middle-class life includes clothes, a house, a few cars, vacation time, maybe an upper-management position, and some money in the bank.

However, depending on the period in history to which we're referring, the term "middle class" has had a variety of meanings—many of which have been and still are quite contradictory. It has referred to the class of people between peasants and nobility, whereas other definitions suggest that the middle class had enough capital to rival nobles. We've clearly come a long way from that meaning today. For example, in

India, the middle class is considered to be those who reside in an owner-occupied property, whereas a blue-collar job makes you middle class in the United States—and in Europe, that makes you a member of the working class.

An important distinction that I'd like to make is my own reference to "middle class" as a mind-set rather than an income level. Someone who makes $1 million a year may still adopt middle-class thinking and actions. It is more of a mentality that creates the trap that will fail you. The middle class is, in large part, a goal that will not provide you with what you truly want. It is "middle"—normal or average—synonymous with the terms we've already deemed as highly unattractive.

But what does middle class mean to most people nowadays? In February 2009, authoritative weekly publication *The Economist* announced that over half the world's population now belongs to this group as a result of rapid growth in emerging countries. The article characterized middle class as having a reasonable amount of discretionary income and not having to live from hand to mouth as the poor do. It was defined as beginning at the point where people have roughly a third of their income left for discretionary spending after paying for basic food and shelter.

However, almost no member of today's middle class has one-third of his or her income left for discretionary income. This group is currently being hammered by something called the middle-class squeeze—a situation in which increases in wages fail to keep up with inflation for middle-income earners. At the same time, the phenomenon fails to have a similar impact on the top wage earners. Add to that the fact that much of the supposed middle class's wealth has come from assuming debt and home equity calculations that were more ink than real money.

Persons belonging to the middle class frequently find that their dependence upon credit—worsened by the collapse of the housing market—prevents them from maintaining a middle-class lifestyle, making downward mobility a threat to counteract aspirations of upward mobility. This is the gravity, resistance, and unexpected conditions I mentioned earlier. This group then experiences middle-class income declining as jobs are lost. And for the first time in our history, we are seeing more men lose jobs than women because higher-paid males are being let go in favor of keeping their less expensive counterparts. At the same time, the prices of necessary items—such as energy, education, housing, and insurance—continue to increase while wages decrease. This kind of squeeze always affects the largest groups of people in a given population. The wealthy don't depend on income and debt, and the poor will receive help for which the middle class don't qualify.

For most people, being middle class means having a reliable job with fair to good pay, consistent health care, a fairly comfortable home in a nice neighborhood, a good education (whatever that means) for one's children, time off for vacations (this is highly valued), and money in a 401(k) that is growing and allowing for a decent retirement. Yet all of this—taken for granted for so long—is now in turmoil, thanks to a housing implosion and credit collapse. The existing middle class is being squeezed and hopes, at best, to hold on to or recover past achievements. This group's average income is steadily decreasing. Its members' jobs are in jeopardy, and their savings and investments have been put at risk. The greatly appreciated vacation of the past will probably be more like a visit to the neighborhood park.

What is the point of me telling you all this? Ask people in the middle class if this feels secure or desirable—and although they may claim that they're grateful not to be "poor," they will likely tell you that they feel more like a member of the working class than the middle class. Consider as well the fact that the dollar is worth less today than it was yesterday and will be worth even less tomorrow. Someone who's making $60,000 a year pays $15,000 in taxes. If that person is lucky, he or she is left with $45,000 a year—which is really worth only $32,000—for a home, schools, insurance, food, car payments, fuel, medical emergencies, vacations, and savings. Does this sound desirable to you? Middle class was a dream sold to countless

Americans as a good goal toward which they should strive. Yet in reality, it is really only close to "good"—and probably better described as a mousetrap with a big fat piece of cheese on it.

I contend that the middle class is the most suppressed, restricted, and confined socioeconomic demographic in the world. Those who desire to be a part of it are compelled to think and act in a certain way where "just enough" is the reward. The idea that one would only have enough to be "comfortable" or "adequately satisfied" is a concept that has been sold—by the educational system, the media, and politicians—to convince an entire population of people to settle instead of strive for abundance. However, it only takes a bit of waking up to discover that it is a promise without fulfillment. Today the wealthiest 5 percent of people control $80 trillion, which is more money than has been created in the history of mankind. If you knew that you had the same energy and creativity to make it to the next level, wouldn't you give it a try?

Exercise

Before you read this chapter, what was your understanding of the middle class?

_____

_____

_____

What are the income levels of the middle class?

_____

_____

_____

What does middle class mean to you now?

_____

_____

_____

12

Obsession Isn't a Disease; It's a Gift

The dictionary defines the term "obsessed" as "the domination of one's thoughts or feelings by a persistent idea, image, or desire." Although the rest of the world tends to treat this mind-set like a disease, I believe that it's the perfect adjective for how you must approach success. To dominate your sector, your goal, dream, or ambition, you must first dominate your every interest, thought, and consideration. Obsession is not a bad thing here; it is a requirement to get where you want to go. In fact, you want to be so fanatical about success that the world knows you will not compromise or go away. And until you become completely obsessed with your mission, no one will take you seriously. Until the world understands that you're not going away—that you are 100 percent committed and have complete and utter conviction and will persist in pursuing your project—you will not get the attention you need and the support you want. In this context, obsession is like a fire; you want to build it so big that people feel compelled to sit around it in admiration. And as with a fire, you have to keep adding wood to sustain the heat and the glow. You obsess over how to keep your fire burning—or it will turn to ashes.

To create a 10X reality, you have to follow up every action with an obsession to see it through to success. You need to stay seriously motivated to take 10X actions every day. Though people take action constantly, we know that much of this isn't the kind of action that's going to get them anywhere. Most are doing nothing or have already given up, and others retreat in an attempt to avoid failure and negative experiences. Huge segments of the population are merely operating at normal levels in order to get by and fit in. Each of these groups lacks the obsession to see their actions all the way through to success. *Most people make only enough effort for it to feel like work, whereas the most successful follow up every action with an obsession to see it through to a reward.*

If you become obsessed with your idea, purpose, or goal, you will become equally addicted to the idea of making it work. Anyone who makes it his or her mission to create long-term, positive 10X survival will have to approach each moment, decision, action, and day with this level of fixation. After all, if your ideas do not excessively preoccupy your own thoughts, then how can you ever expect them to preoccupy the thoughts of others? *Something* has to absorb your thoughts every second of every day—so what should it be? Be obsessed with something. Make your dreams, goals, and mission your mind's and actions' dominant concern!

The word "obsessed" tends to have a negative connotation because many people believe that obsession with something (or someone) is usually destructive or harmful. But show me one person who has achieved greatness without being obsessed on some level. You simply cannot do it. Any individual or group that accomplished something significant was completely obsessed with the idea of it. Whether it was an artist, musician, inventor, businessman, change agent, or philanthropist, their greatness was a result of their fixation.

Someone once asked me if I've always been as obsessed with success and work as I am today. I answered, "Absolutely not!" At first, I was—until about the age of 10. Then I let it go and didn't become obsessed until I was 25. I have remained that way—to some greater or lesser degree—ever since, and I regret those years I was not obsessed with my dreams and goals. I can tell you that my life has gone much better since I've been passionate about my dreams and goals—even when things went wrong.

I recently saw a television interview with Israeli President Shimon Peres. Mr. Peres was 87 years old at the time and had done 900 interviews over the prior 18 months. His obsession with his mission makes him seem youthful and energetic—despite his age. Even those who may not believe in his mission have to admire his commitment to it, which is evidenced by his claim that "work is better than vacation—and it is important to have a purpose to wake up each day." Countless truly successful people agree with the sentiment that their careers do not feel like work but rather something they love to do. That is obsession at its best.

Children are a wonderful example of inherent obsession. They are almost instantly fixated with any task they encounter learning, mimicking, discovering, playing, and utilizing their full energy for whatever captures their interest. Unless some part of their development has been delayed, no child approaches his or her activities without thorough obsession and complete preoccupation of whatever they desire—be it a pacifier, a toy, food, daddy's attention, or an urgent need to be changed. In this way, we see how obsession is a natural human state. It doesn't become a "problem" until a parent, caretaker, teacher—and eventually, society as a whole—begins *suppressing* this fixation. They often make the child feel as if his or her commitment to a goal is wrong rather than something natural and very right! At this point, many children begin to assume that their intense interest in life and discovery—their innate commitment to be fully engaged—is somehow wrong or unnatural. They have essentially been bullied by others—who have long ago given up on their own obsessions—in order to change their behavior. This is when a person moves from higher levels of commitment and action to "average" levels.

Lest you think I'm talking about something with which I have no personal experience, I should tell you that I just had my first child. I will admit that although her obsessive nature rears its head at inconvenient times for me, I *never* want to suppress that. It is my fervent wish that my daughter becomes obsessed with whatever her dreams are, never gives up achieving them, and then spends the rest of her life improving on them! I love the feeling that comes with being obsessed about an idea, and I admire seeing others who are that fanatical. Who isn't moved by the people or groups that go after the things in which they believe with all their heart—who is so consumed by their ideas that they wake up to their dreams each day, work on them all day long, and then go to sleep and dream about them again all night? As soon as other people see the intention, conviction, and commitment in the passionate individual's thoughts, eyes, and movements, they quickly get out of the way. *I suggest that you become obsessed about the things you want; otherwise, you are going to spend a lifetime being obsessed with making up excuses as to why you didn't get the life you wanted.*

It is unfortunate that people with this kind of voracious obsession and fierce drive are categorized as off-balance, work-addicted, obsessive, and a whole litany of other labels. What if the world saw a person's unwavering passion, undying obsession, and a bonfire-like desire to see through his or her goals as gifts rather than as defects or diseases? Wouldn't we all accomplish more? Why do people have to turn a passion for excellence and an obsession to succeed into something negative?

It's interesting, however, that once the obsessed finally do become successful, they're no longer labeled as crazy but instead as geniuses, exceptions to the rule, and extraordinary. What if the world admired, expected, and even demanded that we all operate every single day with an obsessive focus on our goals? What if we punished the people who didn't act with passion and commitment and rewarded those who saw their projects through to the end? Our society would be overwhelmed with inventions, solutions, new products, and increased efficiency. What if the world *encouraged* obsession instead of judging it? What if the only thing standing in the way of your greatness was that you just had to go after everything obsessively, persistently, and as though your life depended on it? Well—it does!

Would human beings have made it into space if a team of people hadn't been obsessed with making it happen? Can a country become great without its leaders being obsessed with greatness? Would any remarkable leader water down his or her dreams and encourage the team to adopt a "take-it-or-leave-it" attitude? Of course not! Do you want your team drugged, lethargic, and robotic or obsessed with a positive outcome and victory? Never cut anything, never dilute greatness, never pull back on your horsepower, and never put a limit on your ambition, drive, and passion. Demand obsession of yourself and all those around you. Never make it wrong to be obsessed; instead, make it your goal. Obsession is what you will need to set 10X goals and to follow them up with 10X actions.

Remember as well that making the goal too small won't allow you to gather the right fuel or take the right amount of action to break through the resistance, competition, and changing conditions. Nothing great will ever happen without someone becoming obsessed with the concept—and then staying obsessed while approaching each task, challenge, and moment as vital, necessary, and a *must*. The ability to be obsessed is not a disease; it is a gift!

Exercise

Write down the names of three obsessed people who did something great.

_____

_____

_____

_____

_____

_____

What good thing do you need to be obsessed about again?

_____

_____

_____

_____

_____

Why is it better to be obsessed than not?

_____

_____

_____

_____

_____

What goal would cause you to become obsessed?

_____

_____

_____

_____

_____

13

Go "All In" and Overcommit

Now that I hopefully have rehabilitated your opinion about the nature of obsession, let's discuss what we have to do to get you to go "all in" on every action and fully commit to every opportunity.

Most people are familiar with the "all-in" concept as a poker term. It's what takes place when a player puts all of his chips at risk and either gets knocked out or doubles up. Though I'm not talking about money or chips here, I'm referring to a much more important bet—your efforts, creativity, energy, ideas, and persistence. Massive action is not like a poker table; you never run out of action chips in life or use up all of your energy and effort by committing yourself. The most valuable chips you have are your mind-set, actions, persistence, and creativity. You can go "all in" with energy as many times as you want—because even if you fail, you can keep going all in!

Most of society discourages the all-in mentality because we are taught to play it safe and not to put everything at risk. We are encouraged to conserve and protect ourselves from losses rather than to go for the big payoff. The giants on this planet are willing to make the big plays. This mind-set is yet again based on the myth that your energy, creativity, and efforts are material things with limited quantities that cannot be replaced. There *are* certain things in life that have limits, but *you* don't unless you impose limits on yourself.

It is vital that you get your head completely reworked about taking action and that you understand that there is no limit to how many times you can continue to take action. You can fail or succeed as many times as you want and then do it over and over again. Also, you can't ever hit it out of the park if you don't initially make contact and swing for the fences, and you will never hit it big if you don't discipline yourself to be all in when you don't take action.

We have all heard the fable of the tortoise and the hare. The implied lesson, of course, is that the tortoise wins because he plods along and takes his time, whereas the hare rushes, becomes tired, and misses his opportunity to win. We're supposed to derive the meaning that we should be tortoises—individuals who approach our goals steadily and slowly. If there was a third player in the fable who had the speed of the hare and the steadfastness of the tortoise, it would smoke them both and have no competition. The fable would then be called *Smoked*. The suggestion here is to approach your goals like the tortoise *and* the hare—by attacking them ruthlessly from the beginning and also staying with them throughout the course of the "race."

Remember: There are no shortages of how many times you can get up and continue! There is no failure unless you quit! It is impossible for you to "use up" all of your energy—or creativity. It is impossible for you to run out of ideas. You'll never lose the ability to come up with new dreams, have more energy, think creatively, look at a situation or event differently, give someone another call, use another tactic, or act with persistence. There will always be another hand, another day—and another chance. If the bank you are working with continues to refill you with new supplies of energy, creativity, and persistence, then why *not* go all in on every hand?

Entrepreneurs and especially salespeople suffer most when they fail to go all in—a topic I discussed in my first book, *Sell to Survive*. Many sales professionals give themselves much more credit for trying to close the deal than they deserve and think they're doing so much more often than they actually are. In reality, most never even ask for the order once, *much less the supposed five times that are necessary*.

My company was recently hired to conduct a "mystery shop" campaign for an international company to identify where the breakdowns in the sales process were occurring. We were trying to collect information on where the franchises needed the most help. We visited more than 500 locations to see what percentage of time the sales force was able to position the client to even ask for an order on the product. To the company's amazement, 63 percent of the locations shopped never even presented the client with a proposal to purchase—much less ask our mystery shopper to buy! This company was about to spend millions on a product training program when in reality, this was not the problem. The franchises and their sales teams feared failure or rejection and never even played a hand—much less went all in.

If a client comes to you or you get a chance to get in front of a client and talk about your product but never present a proposal, I assure you that you will not get the business *100 percent* of the time. Society has successfully taught most of us to play it safe rather than to go all in with every customer and every opportunity. This is perpetuated in the business world with things like closing ratios, which supposedly reflect the success rate of a salesperson. I'll tell you what I do: I am willing to go for it with every customer, every time, and have the lowest closing ratio of everyone but the highest production! All in. I don't care how many times I bust out, I will just reload my chips and play again!

Think about it: What's the worst thing that can happen to you if you just totally go for it? You may lose the customer, but so what? You still have unlimited resources to give it your all with the next client. You have everything to gain and nothing to lose; you simply have to rethink your approach.

This brings me to the topic of overcommitting, another "frowned-upon" and misunderstood issue in business today. How many times have you been told to "undercommit and overdeliver?" I have never heard anything so backward and ridiculous. Let's say you are putting on a Broadway show that you're advertising to the public. Should you announce that you have a mediocre cast with just "average" singing ability—and then wait until opening night to overdeliver? Of course not. This phrase suggests that overcommitting—or, at the very least, *fully* committing—somehow puts you in danger. If you're then not able to deliver as promised, you'll leave the other party dissatisfied. Why not overcommit in your promise—and then exceed by overdelivering as well? Tell everyone about your spectacular Broadway cast, and compel them to see the show for themselves. Overcommit *and* overdeliver!

I find that the greater the commitment I make to a client, the higher my level of delivery naturally becomes. It is as though I'm promising to both them and myself to reach new levels of what I'm able to do for them. The more energy I devote to the markets, my clients, or my family, the more intent I am upon delivering exactly what I said I was going to. This, of course, goes back to acting with 10X effort rather than 1X effort. It's easy for someone to claim to be giving "110 percent" but then fail to fully commit—either because that person is playing it safe or is afraid that he or she won't perform to the level necessary.

A common problem that almost every business faces is the tendency to increase appointments in order to present a product or idea. People who request an appointment aren't willing to overcommit to the person who has to give up his or her valuable time in order to see them. Grand claims, over-commitment, and extreme promises will immediately separate you from the masses—and therefore *force* you to deliver at 10X levels. The only way to increase appointments is to increase the number of people to whom you speak—and then amplify the reasons why they should make time for you.

The same goes for every step of the sales process, whether it involves follow-up, fliers, regular mail, e-mails, social media, phone calls, personal visits, events, meetings, or any other action you take. Overcommit your energy, resources, creativity, and persistence. Know that you are all in on every activity, every time you take action, every day you're in business.

Now, you might worry—as so many people do—about not being able to deliver. And that is certainly a problem; however, as we discussed earlier, you *need* new problems. They're signs that you're making progress and heading in the right direction. Learn to commit first, and figure out how to show up later. Most people simply never bother to perform and instead spend their time trying to wrap their heads around things that may never happen for them. Anyone who doesn't face new problems but who instead grapples with the same old problems his or her whole life isn't moving forward. Simply put: If you are not creating new problems for yourself, then you aren't taking enough action.

You need to face new issues and dilemmas that will challenge you to keep finding and creating solutions. Wouldn't it be nice if you had *too* many people to see at 2 PM or if you had a line outside your restaurant because there were so many people waiting for a table? One of the major differences between successful and unsuccessful people is that the former *look* for problems to resolve, whereas the latter make every attempt to *avoid* them. So remember: Overcommit, be all in, and take massive levels of action followed up by massive amounts of more actions. You will create new problems and deliver at levels that will amaze even you.

Exercise

What does it mean to go "all in"?

_____
_____
_____
_____
_____

Why do most members of society discourage this?

_____
_____
_____
_____
_____

What is the reason why salespeople fail?

_____
_____
_____
_____
_____

Fill in the following: If you ____ commit and ____ deliver, you'll make yourself grow because _____.

Why do we want new problems?

_____
_____
_____
_____
_____

14

Expand—Never Contract

As of the writing of this book, our country is still experiencing very serious economic stress. Unemployment numbers and financial uncertainty are reaching heights not seen since the Great Depression. During major economic contractions like these, the world becomes convinced to reduce, save, be careful, and stay cautious. Although this mind-set focuses on self-preservation and protection of assets, it is the very kind of thinking that will guarantee you never get what you want. And although the majority of the world has entered a state of contraction, small percentages of people and companies are still capitalizing by expanding. These people understand that these times of tightening are unique opportunities to take from those who are taking a defensive posture by reducing spending.

Because contracting is a form of retreating, it violates the concept of the 10X Rule, which demands that you continue to act, produce, and create in massive quantities regardless of the situation or circumstances. I will admit that it can be very difficult and counterintuitive to expand while others are taking protective measures. However, it's an approach you must adopt in order to take advantage of opportunity. Remember: Regardless of what is happening in the world at any given time, most people are not taking massive action. Although there are, of course, times when you must defend, retreat, and conserve, you should only do so for short periods of time—in order to prepare yourself to reinforce and attack again. You would never contract as a continued business effort. Although we frequently seem to hear reports of companies that failed because they expanded too fast, the case for many of them probably wasn't so simple. Most companies fail not because they stay on the offensive but because they don't properly prepare themselves for expansion and cannot dominate the sector.

The idea of constant, unwavering expansion is counterintuitive and even unpopular; however, it will separate you from the rest of the pack more than any other single activity. The task of expanding when others are contracting should not be reduced to some simplistic concept. This is a very difficult discipline to apply in the real world. Yet once you get into the groove of making it your innate method of responding, the ability to continuously, relentlessly attack any activity will give way to forward movement. Any disagreement with this comes because most people only attack to the point where they meet resistance— and then back off. It's kind of like challenging the schoolyard bully and then running away; it always turns out badly. If you approach trials in this way, the market, your clients, and your competition will not believe that you're committed to a persistent attack. Therefore, they will threaten or criticize you—and you will back off. You'll figure that it didn't work—but the only reason why it didn't work is because you didn't stick with it long enough for the market, your clients, and your competition to finally submit to your efforts. Repeated attacks over extended periods of time will *always* be successful.

You must implement the tactic of expansion regardless of whether the economy and those surrounding you encourage you to do so. I say this because we live in a society that promotes contraction most of the time, and when it does support expansion, it is typically too late in the cycle—hence the recent meltdown. News of contraction should serve as an indicator for you to do the contrary. You never want to blindly follow the masses; they are almost always wrong. Instead of following the pack, lead them! The way out is to expand, push, and take action—regardless of what others are saying and doing.

I watched others in my sector cut staff and promotion dollars during this recent recession—which served as a green light for me to augment my own forces. I didn't cut employees or promotional spending. Instead, I increased both. Even though I saw our revenue shrink with the rest of the world's, I opted to cut my own salary as an alternative. I redirected those monies to promote the business, which helped to increase my footprint and take market share from other organizations that were retreating. In fact, I spent more money on advertising, marketing, and promotion in the course of those 18 months than I had in 18 years! I realize how counterintuitive this was. I fully admit that it was scary and that I often second-guessed my actions. Yet I knew that if I could continue to keep pushing forward, I would gain tremendous ground.

Even more important than the money I spent were the demands I made on my staff and myself to repeatedly expand the use of our most valuable resources: energy, creativity, persistence, and contact with our clients. By doing so, we immediately increased production in every area: phone calls, e-mails, e-newsletters, social media posts, personal visits, speaking engagements, teleconferences, webinars, Skype conferences, and the like. Over that year and a half, I published three books, introduced four new sales programs, produced more than 700 segments of training material for a virtual training site, did 600 radio interviews, wrote more than 150 articles or blog entries, and made thousands of personal phone calls. While the rest of the world withdrew, we expanded on every front possible.

Pretty much everyone in the world was convinced that their only saving grace was to save—so they did. It's always intriguing to me that when people start saving money, they immediately begin saving everything else—almost automatically. It is as though the mind is unable to distinguish between saving paper bills or numbers in a bank and conserving energy, creativity, and effort. The whole world held back in its expenditure of both dollars and effort while just a few people expanded. Who do you think came out on top?

People have asked me how—and why—I decided to expand when things were so uncertain. My answer to them was, "I would rather die in expansion than die in contraction. I would rather fail pushing forward than in retreat." Consider this yourself: At which of the four degrees of action introduced in Chapter 7 do *you* choose to operate? If you allow the economy to determine your choice, you will never be in control of your own economy.

The solution? Get off the sofa, get out of your home, and make your way into the market! Get in front of clients, seek out opportunities, and show that you are advancing in the market. Only retreat for brief moments, if necessary, in order to shore up resources so that you can prepare to expand with even more action. Your energy, efforts, creativity, and personality are worth more than the dollars that men create and machines print. And although spending money is the most common way for businesses to expand, it is certainly not the only way—and is not nearly as valuable as taking 10X actions consistently and persistently.

Remember 10X, baby. You want to expand with the goal of dominating your sector and getting attention by taking massive action. Only then will you be able to expand your contacts, influences, connections, and visibility with the goal of creating new problems. You will then continue to expand until everyone—including your supposed competitors—knows you are the dominant 10X player and always associates your name with what you do.

Exercise

What are some ways you can expand that only require
energy and creativity, not money?

_____
_____
_____
_____
_____
_____

When have you ever benefited from contraction?

_____
_____
_____
_____
_____
_____

When have you expanded your efforts? What results did
you see?

_____
_____
_____
_____
_____
_____
_____

15

Burn the Place Down

Once you take 10X actions and start getting traction, you must continue to add wood to your fire until you either start a brushfire or a bonfire—or burn the place down. Don't rest, and don't stop—ever. I learned this the hard way after achieving a lot of success and then resting on my laurels. This is a commonly made mistake. Do *not* do it! Keep stacking wood until the fire is so hot and burns so brightly that not even competitors or market changes can put your fire out. Your fire has to continue to be stoked, and that means more wood, more fuel, and in your case, more actions. Once you start operating like this, it will become almost second nature to continue—because you are going to be winning. It's easiest and most natural to continue taking massive actions when you are winning—and winning is only possible with massive actions.

When you begin to "heat things up," you'll quickly become aware—even obsessed—with the possibilities before you and will start to see new levels of positive results. Your actions will start to perpetuate themselves like a flywheel that, once it gets going, continues going. Newton talked about the law of inertia: An object in motion continues in motion. Keep taking action until you can't stop your forward momentum. You might even find yourself operating on less sleep and food because you are literally subsisting on your adrenaline generated by your victories. It will be about this time that people start offering you admiration—and then advice. Be particularly wary of those who suggest you have "done enough" or who advise you to take a rest or vacation. Now is not the time for rest and celebration; it's time for more action. Andy Grove, one of Intel Corporation's first employees, coined the saying, "Only the paranoid survive." Although I'm not recommending that you spend your entire career in a state of paranoia, I do believe that you must stay committed to taking action. Even after achieving successes along the way, continue to take more actions in order to exceed your goals. The time to celebrate or take vacations will come. Right now, you must keep adding wood until the fire is burning so hot that no one—and nothing—can put out your successes.

One of the problems with success is that it demands continuous attention. Success tends to bless those who are most committed to giving it the most attention. It's somewhat like a lawn or garden; no matter how green it gets or beautiful the flowers, you must continue to tend to it. You have to keep mowing, trimming, edging, watering, and planting; otherwise, your grass will turn brown and your flowers will die. That is the case for success as well. There is *no* retreating for those who want to create and keep it. It is a myth to believe that the successful get to "kick back" and stop making the very efforts that have brought them fulfillment in the first place.

Always keep the four actions—doing nothing, retreating, taking an average amount of action, and taking massive action— in mind. The 10X Rule means you are going to create success in quantities great enough that you are constantly in total control. The wannabes and people who get close are the ones who quit adding wood and then backed off. Massive action is designed to move you past your peers and off the "treadmill." The best way to quit worrying about competition and uncertainty is to build a fire so large and so hot that everyone in the world—even your competition—comes to sit by *your* fire for warmth. Keep in mind that most competition is created by those who are unwilling to operate at the higher levels of action, who merely imitate others' efforts. There can never be enough wood on your fire. You can never take too much action or accumulate too much success. There is no such thing as being talked or written about excessively, being covered too frequently, receiving too much authority, or working too much. These are simply claims that mediocre people make in order to justify their own decisions to be happy with the status quo.

How can you ever take too much action when you have an endless ability to create new actions? Look at the big players on this planet. None of them ever "runs out" of energy, efforts, people, ideas, or resources. They enjoy the gifts of abundance because they create abundance in their enterprises. So instead of resenting them, admire and emulate them. If you do, you'll find that the more you commit to new actions, the more creative you will become. It is as though your imagination opens up, and new possibilities just pour from it. It's not even necessarily the creativity that is so brilliant but the ability to take massive action that it prompts.

I recently met with a very high-profile PR firm in Los Angeles whose members suggested that I was in danger of being "overexposed"—something I thought was an extremely strange concept. The notion of overexposure—the idea that you can see or hear too much about someone—is based on the concept that a person doesn't continue to generate new ideas and products. The underlying belief is that an overexposed person or product will somehow lose its value. But consider the following: Coca-Cola is known by almost everyone on planet Earth. You can find the company's products in almost every store, bar, airplane, and hotel in the world.

Is it overexposed? Should it hide its products? Should the company hold back in fear that Coca-Cola will lose its value because too many people are hearing about and using it? This seems to be a fairly ridiculous way of thinking. And there are countless other examples of products and companies that prove this point—Microsoft, Starbucks, McDonald's, Wells Fargo, Google, Fox TV, Marlboro, Walgreens, Exxon, Apple, Toyota—and even some athletic and celebrity personalities. Although overexposure is usually not the problem, obscurity certainly can be. Remember: If you don't know (or know about) me, then it doesn't matter how good my product is or how low my price is. And even if this *were* the case, I would rather be overexposed than face obscurity.

The sad but true fact is that most people don't even get in the neighborhood of building a bonfire. They're either miseducated, socially programmed to settle for less, or fear that their actions will somehow get "out of control." I promise you that this will not happen. You must build your fire so big and so hot that you not only burn the house down but incinerate everything in your path. Go all the way—and then keep going until your fire burns so hot that people stand in admiration of your ability to take action. Don't worry about the resistance you're afraid you'll face from either the market or your competitors. They'll get right out of your way once they see that you're a force to be reckoned with.

Exercise

What is the fire you have always wanted to start and add wood to?

_____
_____
_____
_____
_____
_____
_____

What three things could you do to add wood to that fire?

_____
_____
_____
_____
_____
_____
_____

Who can you get support from in order to continue stoking your fire?

_____
_____
_____
_____
_____
_____
_____

16

Fear Is the Great Indicator

Sooner or later, you will experience fear when you start taking new actions at new levels. In fact, if you aren't, then you're probably not doing enough of the right things. Fear isn't bad or something to avoid; conversely, it's something you want to seek and embrace. Fear is actually a sign that you are doing what's needed to move in the right direction.

An absence of concerns signals that you are only doing what's comfortable for you—and that will only get you more of what you have right now. As strange as it may sound, you *want* to be scared until you have to push yourself to new levels to experience fear again. In fact, the only thing that scares me is a complete lack of fear.

What is fear anyway? Does it exist? Is it real? I know it *feels* real when you are experiencing it, but admit it: Most of the time, what you fear doesn't even occur. It's been said that

FEAR stands for **F**alse **E**vents **A**ppearing **R**eal, which aptly implies that most of what you're afraid of doesn't ever come to pass. Fear, for the most part, is provoked by emotions, not rational thinking. And in my humble estimation, emotions are wildly overrated—and the scapegoat many people use for their failure to act. But regardless of whether you agree with my opinion on emotions, you must reframe your understanding of fear and use it as a reason to move forward rather than as an excuse to stop or retreat. Use this frequently avoided feeling as a green light to signal you to what you *should* do!

Chances are that when you were a child, you found fear in irrational things—the boogeyman under the bed, for example. It was an indicator to check your closet and the dark corners of your room to see what was lurking. But as all children eventually find, the boogeyman does not exist anywhere except in your head. Adults have their own "boogeymen"—the unknown, rejection, failure, success, and so on. And these boogeymen should be a sign to take action as well. For example, if you're afraid to call on a client, then it's a sign that you should call that client. Fear of speaking with the boss is an indication that you should march into his office and ask for a moment of his time. Fear of requesting the client's business means that you *must* ask for the business—and then keep asking.

The 10X Rule compels you to separate yourself from everyone else in the market. And you do that by—as I emphasized earlier—doing what others *refuse* to do. Only in this way will you distinguish yourself and dominate your sector. Everyone experiences fear on some level, and because the marketplace is composed of people interacting with both products and one another, the market will face fear in the same way that you and your peers do. But rather than seeing fear as a sign to run—as most other people in the market will do—it must become your indicator to *go*.

I handle this dilemma myself by omitting time from the equation—since time is what drives fear. The more time you devote to the object of your apprehension, the stronger it becomes. So starve the fear of its favorite food by removing time from its menu. For example, let's say that John needs to make a call to a client, a task that immediately causes him to feel anxiety. So rather than picking up the phone and making the call immediately, he gets a cup of coffee and thinks about what he is going to do. His lengthy contemplation only causes his fear to grow, as he imagines all the ways the call could go badly and all the potentially terrible things that could happen. If confronted, he's likely to claim that he needs to "prepare" before he makes the call. But preparation is merely an excuse for those who haven't trained properly—and who use it as a reason to justify their last-minute reluctance. John needs to take a deep breath, pick up the phone, and just *make the call*. Last-minute preparation is just another way to feed the fear that will only get stronger as time is added. Nothing happens without action.

Fear doesn't just tell you *what* to do; it also tells you when to do it. Ask yourself what time it is at any point in the day, and the answer is always the same: *now*. The time is always now—and when you experience fear, it's a sign that the best time to take action is at that very moment. Most people will not follow through with their goals when enough time has passed from the inception of their idea to actually doing something about it; however, if you remove time from your process, you'll be ready to go. There's simply no other choice than to act. There's no need to prepare. It's too late for that once you've gotten this far.

Now, the only thing that will make a difference is *action*. Everyone has had the experience of failing to do something they wanted to do. Perhaps by the time you got yourself "ready" to do something, someone else had taken action— and now you're regretting it. Failure comes in many forms; it occurs whether you act or not. Regardless of the outcome, I would say that it's far preferable to fail while doing something than to fail by over-preparing while someone else walks up and scoops up your dreams.

This scenario occurs in business every day. People give their fears much more time than they deserve. They wait to make the personal visit or phone call, write the e-mail, or present their proposal because they're afraid of the outcome. Countless individuals share the same excuses for why it is "not a good time" to take action. The client is leaving town. The client just got back into town. It's the end of the month or the beginning of the month. The clients have been in meetings all day. They are about to go into meetings. They just bought something. They don't have the budgets. They are cutting back. Business is bad. There's been a change in management or staff. I don't want to "bug" them. They never return my phone calls anyway. No one else can sell them. They are unrealistic. I don't know what to say. I am not ready yet. I just called them yesterday . . . and on and on.

All the excuses in the world won't change one simple fact: that fear is a sign to do whatever it is you fear—and do it quickly. My wife tells me all the time that I "seem fearless." The truth is actually quite the contrary; I am scared most of the time. However, I refuse to feed my fear with time and allow it to get stronger. I opt instead to get things done quickly. I've learned that it's simply better for me to take this approach. You will experience the same when you're finally able to take the plunge and do what you fear. In fact, you'll be amazed at how much stronger you become and how much more confident you are to do new things.

Taking massive action quickly and repeatedly will ensure that you appear fearless in the marketplace. The person who takes action on whatever he or she fears the most will be the person who advances his or her cause the most. Let the rest of the marketplace submit to anxiety and prepare unnecessarily for False Events Appearing Real. You've got a job to do.

Fear is one of the most disabling emotions a human being can experience. It immobilizes people, and often, it ultimately prevents them from going for their goals and dreams. Everyone fears something in life; however, it's what we each do with that fear that distinguishes us from others. When you allow fear to set you back, you lose energy, momentum, and confidence—and your fears will only grow.

Have you ever watched some kind of performer "eat fire"? It appears that the trick here is to completely exhaust the oxygen that the fire requires for life. Pull away too early, and oxygen refuels the fire—which will then, of course, burn you. The same is true with fear. If you back off from it even the slightest bit, you give it the oxygen it needs to stay alive. So commit yourself entirely, remove time from the equation— and you will snuff out your fears and be able to take more action.

Eat your fears; don't feed them by backing off or giving them time to grow. Learn to look for and use fear so that you know exactly what you need to do to overcome it and advance your life. Every successful person I know of has used fear as an indicator to determine which actions will provide the greatest return. I use it in my own life, every chance I get, to remain aware that I am growing and expanding myself. If you aren't experiencing fear, you are not taking new actions and growing. It's as simple as that. It does not take money or luck to create a great life; it requires the ability to move past your fears with speed and power. Fear, like fire, is not something from which you should pull away. Rather, it should be used to fuel the actions of your life.

Exercise

What are your three biggest fears?

_____
_____
_____
_____
_____
_____
_____
_____

Whom do you fear contacting who could help you or improve your business?

_____
_____
_____
_____
_____
_____
_____
_____

What did you learn about fear in this chapter?

_____
_____
_____
_____
_____
_____
_____
_____

17

The Myth of Time Management

I should begin this chapter by admitting that I do not consider myself a great manager by any means. Neither have I been a great planner. In fact, I've never even written a business plan. However, I've always been able to effectively manage myself well enough to build multiple companies from scratch. Time management has never been something that I considered valuable, even though I do spend time on those things that I think are most valuable.

I often receive questions about time management and balance in my seminars. I have found throughout my career that the people who are most concerned with time management and balance in their lives are the ones who believe in the notion of "shortages" that we discussed in an earlier chapter. Most don't even know how much time is available to them or what tasks are most necessary to accomplish in that time.

If you don't know how much time you have—or need—then
how on earth can you expect to manage and balance it?

The first thing you must do is make success your duty
by setting distinct and definitive priorities. I can't do this for
you, of course; everyone's priorities are different. However, if
success is a main concern for you, then I would suggest you
spend most of your time doing things that will create success.
Of course, I don't know what success means in your life. It
could involve a variety of people and things: finances, family,
happiness, spirituality, physical or emotional well-being—or,
if you're like me, all of them! And remember—it *can* be all of
them. I personally am not interested in balance; I am interested in abundance in every area. I don't think I should have
to sacrifice one in favor of another. Successful people think
in terms of "all," whereas unsuccessful people tend to place
limits on themselves. They may believe that "If I am rich,
I can't be happy" or "If I thrive in my career, then I won't have
time to be a good father, husband, or spiritual individual." In
fact, it's interesting to notice that the people who put limits on
what is available to them are also most inclined to talk about
"balance." However, this is a flawed manner of thinking that
neither time management nor balance will resolve.

As far as I'm concerned, it's pointless for people to
worry about time management and balance. The question
they should be asking is "How can I have it all in abundance?" Successful people have attained the things they
desire in quantities so great that no one can take them away.
And how can a person consider him- or herself successful
if he or she isn't happy? What happiness is there in being
unable to pay the bills or provide for your family or worry
about your future? The moment you achieve one goal you've
set for yourself, then it's time to establish a new target. Quit
thinking in terms of either/or and start thinking in terms of
all and everything.

As I was writing this, a client sent me a message asking,
"Do you ever rest?" I jokingly wrote him back within seconds,

"NEVER!" I do, of course—like every other human being. However, I also know how much time is available to me, what my priorities are, and that it is my duty, obligation, and responsibility to go after them in the time I have. I challenge you to keep track of how you're spending your available time, perhaps in a journal. Most people have no clue what they are doing with their time but still complain that they don't have enough.

Every single person has 168 hours in a week, and based on a typical 40-hour work week, the average U.S. employee is only productive 37.5 of those 168 hours (30 minutes for lunch each day). And it's pretty unlikely that most people actually work this entire 37.5 hours. In fact, the average individual spends 22.3 percent of his or her available time at work, 33.3 percent asleep, and then 16.6 percent in front of a TV or online—and those comparisons assume that the person spends 100 percent of his or her time at work actually working! Then these very same people worry about balance and time management. But an imbalance is always going to occur when you don't do enough with the time you have.

While most people claim to value time, many don't seem to know very much about it. Who creates time? Do you create your own time, or does someone else do that? What can you do to create more time? What does the expression "time is money" mean? How do you treat time to make sure your time is money? What is the most important thing that you should do with your time? All of these questions are worthy of consideration and require your attention in order for you to maximize time.

Let's assume that you have 75 years to live; that's approximately 657,000 hours, or 39,420,000 minutes, in this lifetime. Take any given day of the week; you have an average of 3,900 Mondays, Tuesdays, Wednesdays, etc. Now—here's the scary part—if you are 37 years old, then you have only 1,950 Wednesdays left. What if you had only $1,950 left to your name? Would you watch it slip away, or would you do whatever you could to increase it? I believe that I can do more with 1,950 hours than most people can. The only way to increase time is to get more done in the time you have. If I get 15 phone calls done in 15 minutes and you get 15 calls done in one hour, then I have essentially created 45 minutes for myself. In this way, the 10X Rule makes it possible to multiply time. If I hire someone and pay that person $15 an hour to make 15 calls every 15 minutes, then I just duplicated my efforts—and my time becomes money.

To really understand, manage, maximize, and squeeze every opportunity out of the time you have, you have to fully understand and appreciate how much of it you have available to you. You must first take control of your time—not allow others to do so. If you listen to people discuss the topic of time—especially in regards to the amount they have at work—you'll probably hear a lot of complaining. People act as though work is something to *get through*, yet in reality, they spend very little of their time even doing it. *Most people only work enough so that it feels like work, whereas successful people work at a pace that gets such satisfying results that work is a reward.* Truly successful people don't even call it work; for them, it's a passion. Why? Because they do enough to win!

An easy way to achieve balance is to simply *work harder* while you are at the office. This won't just leave you with more time; it will allow you to experience the rewards of your job and make it feel less like work and more like success. Try to take this approach: Be grateful to go to work, and see how much you can get done in the time you have. Make it a race, a challenge—make it fun.

The first thing to do when managing time and seeking balance is to decide what is important to you. In which areas do you most want to achieve success and in what quantities? Write those down in order of importance. Then determine the total amount of time you have available and decide where you are going to allot time to each of these endeavors. Another vital thing to do: Log how you are spending your time daily—and

I mean every single second. This will allow you to see all the ways in which you waste your time—the little habits and activities that in no way contribute to your success. Any action that is not adding wood to your fire would be considered wasteful—think Xbox, online poker, watching television, napping, drinking, taking smoking breaks—the potential list is endless. Brutal, isn't it? Yes, it is—but if you don't manage your time, I promise that you will waste it.

Of course, things will change throughout the course of your life and career. You get older. You achieve and then generate new goals. Different things and people enter your world. All of these changes require that you continue to modify your priorities. For example, I listened for years to parents who told me that I didn't understand how to balance work with family life because I didn't have children of my own. Well, I recently had my first child—most assuredly an event that demands more of my time—and was able to experience this for myself. What I found was not a problem with balance or work but rather a solution based on priorities.

My daughter merely gave me another reason to create success—not an excuse to avoid working more. She is sheer motivation for me to do well because now I'm doing it for her as well as for myself. You cannot blame your family for keeping you from creating the success you deserve. They should be the reason why you *want* to succeed!

It might seem difficult, but there are ways to make it work. Get yourself and your family members on a schedule that allows you to do those things that are a priority for you. For example, my solution was to add one hour to each of my days in order to spend time with my daughter. My wife and I met and created a schedule that would allow me to have time with my daughter and my wife—and not negatively impact the work schedule that provides for our financial success. The first thing my wife and I did was build our daughter's sleep schedule around our priorities. We agreed that I would get up one hour earlier each day and take my daughter on an outing each morning. This would ensure that I would have quality time when I'm home with my daughter before I go to the office and become consumed by the day's events. It also would allow my wife some extra time to sleep. I have been doing this since my daughter was about 6 months old, and it works beautifully. I take her on errands with me—such as going to the local grocery store each morning and introducing her to the people who work there. When I get back from our outing, the rest of the day is mine to produce in the business world uninterrupted. Because I get my daughter up so early, we are then in a position to put her to bed before 7 PM. Then my wife and I are able to spend quality time together as a couple.

We understand that this system will continue to change as my daughter grows up and that alterations will have to be made. However, the point is that we are controlling our time rather than just haphazardly trying to manage it. Our decision to set priorities and commit to a solution lets us be the bosses of our own time. The busier you become, the more you have to manage, control, and prioritize. Although I certainly don't have some scientific formula that will magically make this easier, I can tell you one thing: If you start with a commitment to success and then agree to control time, you will create an agenda that accommodates all you want.

You have to decide how you are going to use your time. You must command, control, and squeeze every second out of it in order to increase your footprint and dominate the marketplace. Get everyone necessary—your family, colleagues, associates, employees—to recognize and agree upon which priorities are most important. If you don't do this, you will have people with different agendas pulling you in all sorts of directions. My schedule works for me because everyone in my life—from my wife to the people who work with me—knows what is most important to me and understands how I value time. This allows us to handle everything else that comes our way.

In our culture, we're frequently encouraged to "slow down, relax, take it easy, find balance" and just "be happy" with where we are and what we have. Although this can sound great in theory, it can be very difficult for people who abandon every decision to be in control of their lives. Most people can't simply "relax and take it easy"—since they never do enough to free themselves of the meager existence that comes as a result of mediocre actions. Work should provide a purpose, a mission, and a sense of accomplishment. These things are vital to every single person's mental, emotional, and physical well-being. People who promote the new age, esoteric advice to "take it slow" are encouraging a mind-set that isn't doing anyone any good. Consider the types of traits this thinking has created in people: laziness, procrastination, a lack of urgency, sloth, a tendency to blame others, irresponsibility, entitlement, and the expectation that it's up to someone else to solve our problems.

Wake up! No one is going to save you. No one is going to take care of your family or your retirement. No one is going to "make things" work out *for* you. The only way to do so is to utilize every moment of every day at 10X levels. This will ensure that you accomplish your goals and dreams. Happiness, security, confidence, and fulfillment come from utilizing your gifts and energy to achieve whatever you've decided is success for you. And it requires every bit of your time, which is yours—and only *yours*—to control.

Exercise

How much time are you at work each day?

_____

_____

_____

_____

_____

_____

How much time do you spend on wasteful activities every day (e.g., watching television, smoking, drinking, oversleeping, getting coffee, having lunches or meetings with no business opportunities)?

_____

_____

_____

_____

_____

What are some of your own time wasters?

_____

_____

_____

_____

_____

What has this chapter taught you about time?

_____

_____

_____

_____

_____

18

Criticism Is a Sign
of Success

Although getting criticized is certainly not the best feeling in the world, I have great news: Receiving criticism is a surefire sign that you are well on your way. Criticism is not something that you want to avoid; rather, it's what you must expect to come your way once you start hitting it big.

Criticism is defined as the judgment of the merits and faults of the work or actions of one individual by another. Although "criticizing" does not necessarily mean "to imply fault," the word is often taken to mean prejudice or disapproval. The dictionary fails to include the following helpful bit of information: When you start taking the right amount of action and therefore creating success, criticism is often not far behind.

Of course, most people don't like being criticized. However, I've found that it comes as a natural result of getting attention. This may be why some people avoid attention in the first place—as an attempt to dodge judgment. However, there's no way to achieve serious levels of success without getting some attention. Yes, people will eye you and make it clear that they disapprove of what you're doing. Let's face it: No matter what choices you make in life, someone is going to criticize you somewhere along the way. Wouldn't you rather receive it from people who are jealous of your success than from your family, boss, or bill collectors for not taking enough action?

When you start taking enough action, it won't be long before you're judged by people who aren't taking any. If you're generating substantial success, people will start to pay attention to you. Some will admire you, some will want to learn from you, but unfortunately, most will envy you. These are the people whose excuses for not doing enough will morph into reasons why what you are doing is wrong.

You need to expect and anticipate this as one of the signs of success. It will come when you start really cranking at 10X levels—often before your accomplishment is even evident. Beware: This criticism can come in many forms. It may first show up as advice from others: "Why are you spending so much energy on that one client? He never buys anything" or "You should enjoy life more! It's not all work, you know." These are the kinds of things that people say to you to make themselves feel better—because your abundance highlights their deficiency. Remember: Success is not a popularity contest. It is your duty, obligation, and responsibility.

A buddy of mine who is in the fence business in Louisiana once admitted to me, "Grant, I don't want attention. The minute I get it, competitors start coming after me. I want to fly under the radar so no one knows what I'm doing." Although that's certainly one way to approach success, you can't "fly under the radar" for too long and expect to ever make it to the top. Laying low in order to avoid attention (and consequently, criticism) probably means that you're holding yourself back to some degree. Your fear of being attacked is keeping you from going for it completely. However, once the naysayers realize and acknowledge that you aren't going away—and that your success is something they should imitate, not judge—they will give up and find someone else to pick on.

Weak and overwhelmed individuals respond to others' success by attacking it. The moment you elect to dominate or acquire territory, you run the risk of becoming a target for these people. You see this in politics constantly; when neither side has a real solution, they merely criticize and lay into one another—and that doesn't do anyone any good. Criticism of any individual or group should signal to the recipient that the person flinging mud is threatened by the entity he or she is belittling. People who habitually disparage others like this usually do not have solutions to their situation—except to degrade other players.

The only way to handle criticism is to foresee it as an element of your success formula. Much like fear, it's a sign that you are making the right moves in the right volumes, getting enough attention, and making enough of a splash. One of my clients recently called my company to complain that my staff had been following up with him too aggressively. I called to ask him what the problem was. After listening to him malign my employees for doing what was essentially their job, I said, "Knock it off. They're simply doing what they know is right because they know we can help you. The fact that you haven't made a decision to move forward and pull the trigger is what should be criticized here—but I will refrain from doing so because it won't do either of us any good. Now, let's stop the negativity and do something positive to move your company forward." I then rewarded my staff for aggressively following up with the client. Receiving complaints about "too much follow-up" is an indication that my staff is moving in the right direction. I refused to allow this client's protests to stop us and supported my staff in their efforts. We all understand that criticism is part of the success cycle, and I won't apologize for any employee of mine who is seeking success. And in case you were wondering—we *did* close the deal. This very same client now tells people with admiration and praise that "those guys follow up like maniacs."

When I finished college, I got a full-time sales job rather than taking a position in the area in which I had received my degree. Within a couple of years, my sales results had taken me to the top 1 percent of all the salespeople in that industry—and way ahead of the people with whom I worked directly. And if you think they didn't criticize me—well, think again. Of course they did! They made jokes about me, poked fun, tried to distract me, and even tried to convince me to cease the very actions that had gotten me to where I was. That is what lower performers do; they make others wrong for doing what is necessary in order to make themselves feel okay about doing nothing! The highest performers—the winners—respond by studying successful people and duplicating success. They train themselves to reach top performers' levels. Because the lower performers are not willing to step up and take responsibility to increase their production, they can only seek to tear down those who are performing at higher levels.

When my book *If You're Not First, You're Last* hit the *New York Times* best-seller list, some of my supposed competitors immediately began criticizing me. One person called the book's title "arrogant." Another asked, "Who does Cardone think he is?" Yet another suggested that I was "getting too big for [my] own good." One person even called me to tell me to get a new editor because he claimed that the grammar was wrong. Did I pay attention to any of these comments? Not for a second. I had a *New York Times* best-seller!

From what I can tell, criticism precedes admiration and—like it or not—goes hand in hand with success. Keep pouring on the success, and sooner or later, the very same people who were putting you down will be admiring you for what you have done. Those who initially judged your actions will later be singing your praises—just as long as you take the criticism as a sign of your growing success and keep the accelerator on your actions at 10X. After all, what better way to retaliate against criticism than to keep succeeding?

Exercise

What have you learned about criticism now?

_____
_____
_____
_____
_____
_____
_____
_____

What criticisms would you most like to hear from people?

_____
_____
_____
_____
_____
_____
_____
_____

Give three examples of when you have seen people go from criticizing others to admiring them.

_____
_____
_____
_____
_____
_____
_____

CHAPTER

19

Customer Satisfaction Is the Wrong Target

The topic of criticism provides an appropriate segue into a discussion about the overused and abused concept of *customer satisfaction*. One of the first protests I hear from people to whom I promote the idea of 10X actions is their concern that customer satisfaction will be damaged. They worry that if they and their company push too much or become overly aggressive, they'll somehow hurt their brand's reputation in the marketplace. Although I suppose that's possible, it's much more likely—due to the overabundance of products and organizations available today—that no one will even know about you or your company or notice your brand in the first place. The board of trustees of a national cable channel I was working with became concerned that a new show that the executives were very excited about did not fit the network's brand. I told them, "If you don't start bringing TV

135

to people's homes that is current and relevant and that people have to tune in to, you ain't going to have a brand to defend." When you fail to find supporters, establish customers, secure investors, and close the deal because you fail to do whatever it takes to get the job done and then you hide under the excuse of protecting brand and customer satisfaction, you'd just as soon have a shovel in your hand and dig your own grave.

Customer service is the wrong target; increasing customers is the right target. This doesn't mean customer satisfaction isn't important. Everyone knows that customers have to be satisfied and happy in order for them to return and give positive word of mouth. If your service or product or investment isn't built to satisfy, then you are a criminal, and this book will only land you in jail sooner. Make your primary focus commanding attention and *generating* customers before you worry about making them happy.

Let me explain simply. Customer satisfaction doesn't concern me very much! Why? Because I know that we over-deliver to our clients and provide customer service that is well beyond "satisfactory." We overdeliver to every client, and we never say no until we absolutely have to. We don't even talk about customer satisfaction in my office. We do talk a lot about how to get more customers because attracting customers to our program is the only way to increase customer satisfaction. You get it. Increasing customer satisfaction is impossible without increasing customers. Whether someone signs up for our free tip of the week or buys a book for $30, an audio program for $500, or a long-term training contract for $1 million, we always overdeliver what is expected. I only concern myself with getting more customers, then I overdeliver to my clients.

I am most worried about noncustomer satisfaction; that is, the people who are dissatisfied because they do not have my product and may not even know that they are unhappy. I know that the only dissatisfied clients we can have are those who don't have my products or who have them and are not using them correctly. We talk about how getting our clients to increase their usage of our material, systems, and processes is the only way to increase customer satisfaction. Not getting a client or having the client use your products incorrectly are bigger "outpoints" than most of the ways that customer satisfaction is thought of. A customer getting the package a day late is an issue and should be handled, but the client who never buys your product suggests that you have a real serious customer satisfaction problem because you never made that person a customer. The first problem you can easily fix. The second one will kill you.

I seek out clients who are qualified to do business with us. I then attend to that individual or company until they agree to hire me, knowing that until they get my product or service, they can't be satisfied. This isn't a pitch. This is what I believe to be true. The attainment of the customer is paramount to customer satisfaction, and customer satisfaction cannot exist without a customer! The attainment of the customer is the most important thing to me. Same thing in relationships: first it is getting the wife, then it is keeping her happy, then it is growing the family, and then looking at new ways to keep everyone happy. What was most important? Getting the wife was paramount to wife satisfaction.

It is impossible for a company to create success by just focusing on customer satisfaction. I believe that the trend of focusing on customer satisfaction has been detrimental to customer acquisition. Companies become so consumed about their current customers' "satisfaction" that many are failing to aggressively acquire and expand their market share.

Customer service is a business term meant to measure how the products and services that companies supply meet—or exceed—customer expectations after the purchase. This assessment is supposedly a key differentiator between the brands customers follow loyally and those that they abandon entirely. Yet most places I go into never service me enough before the sale to ever acquire me as a customer in the first place.

Executives tout the importance of customer service from their ivory towers, yet they forget to promote the attainment of the customer to begin with. Most products don't get my attention so completely that I'm compelled to purchase them without the assistance of the company. Unfortunately, most salespeople never bother to ask the customer to buy when given an opportunity, and then they fail to follow up. Thus, they never make a client.

We do mystery shopping campaigns for companies and have validated this over and over. The biggest problem with companies is that they never make a customer in the first place! If you have a subpar offering—a product that doesn't do what you state it will and that makes people feel like they've been cheated after purchase—the marketplace will dispose of you sooner rather than later. But most people don't fail because their offering is inferior or they have a poor product. Most people fail because they never get enough customers!

Does Starbucks offer the very best customer service and coffee available? I don't know. I do know that the company has made a serious investment in making it easy and convenient to buy its coffee. Is Starbucks concerned about people standing in line too long and getting the right coffee and being greeted? Of course. But I assure you the company is concerned first with the acquirement of the client. Does Google provide the best search engine and the best customer experience and service? Does it look to improve the experience? Certainly. But first it dominates the space so clearly and gets so much attention that it's the first site used. What's my point here? Brands that truly deliver customer satisfaction do not talk about customer *service*; they focus on customer *acquisition*. Emerging organizations first need people to know about them, then do everything they can to make them happy. Remember, customer satisfaction cannot exist without a customer first.

American corporations have become so obsessed with "customer satisfaction" that they've lost sight of the first—and most vital—factor: customer acquisition! "Keep the main thing the main thing," as they say in the South. Customer satisfaction shouldn't be an initiative but something so inherent to an organization that all of its attention is focused on customer acquisition. To garner the attention of a potential customer or market and then fail to capitalize on creating a user of your products and services makes no sense and is the most expensive of mistakes. Yet that is what happens with far too many organizations.

Let's say that a company successfully gets my attention long enough that I consider its products but then doesn't do enough to earn my business and "shut me down" (i.e., make me a customer). Not being a customer makes it impossible for me to become a satisfied customer. I am just saying don't put the cart before the horse. Notice how executives become concerned about customer satisfaction and then start initiatives to conduct customer satisfaction surveys of the individuals who became customers—and completely ignore surveying those who did not become customers. This is a huge miss and a great example of an "only practice" (discussed in chapter 10) that will show you immediately how to acquire more customers. In addition to surveying those you acquired, garnering input from those who didn't buy will disclose much more to the company about true customer satisfaction! Don't you want to find out *why* you didn't acquire the business? You think you didn't satisfy a customer and therefore never made one? Most companies fail not due to lack of quality in their product, service, or their offering. They fail because they don't take enough strategic actions to acquire the support—the client—in the first place. That is why I suggest that customer satisfaction is the wrong target—because you don't even get the opportunity to "satisfy" someone who never evolves into a customer.

My point here is not to negate customer satisfaction after acquisition but to shift your attention back to acquisition. Also understand that it is impossible to somehow completely prevent customer complaints. There are, of course, measures you can take to improve your product or service. But when dealing with human beings, you are going to face complaints and dissatisfaction. It's just that simple. The best you can do is resolve complaints and dissatisfaction when they emerge (and they will—I promise) and treat them as opportunities to be in communication with your clients. What you need is more people interacting with your product or service and the company. Yes, complaints will increase when dealing with human beings—but so will praise. Increase the number of users of your product or service through massive action, not through massive initiatives that cause your people to back off from the acquisition in the first place.

I launched my first company under the naive impression that I would work with a handful of clients and really concentrate my attention on them (thereby eliciting great customer satisfaction). I assumed that this would give me an advantage in the market and allow me to deliver quality service and really make a difference. And although it was a nice idea, it just didn't work out that way. First of all, this plan didn't put me on a scale necessary to build a business with a wide reach to get me attention, and I fell way short of dominance, not to mention the cash flow necessary to continue to support clients. Just as important, it didn't allow me to share my information with enough of the successful people.

When I finally got my thinking to the right levels and committed to expanding my footprint and taking on 10 times more clients, I multiplied my exposure—tenfold—and increased the number of successful people and companies I had been avoiding. I shifted my focus to monumental quantities instead of just serving a handful of clients, which enhanced my ability to spread the word about myself and my company to a growing number of people. The grumbles I received did intensify— right along with the compliments I received. In fact, I enjoyed more successes than I suffered failures because I was exposed to greater numbers of people using my material. Augmenting the numbers of attendees at my seminars and workshops amplified the number of quality clients I had—and expanded the number of individuals who were exposed to my ideas and techniques. More people were talking about my methodologies among their associates, who would then spread the word to people *they* knew, and so on. The more people talked about me, the more I was able to expand my footprint, get more attention, acquire more customers—and *then* create more customer satisfaction. Think about it like this: Would Facebook and Google be better off if they provided their services to only a few people? If they would, I wouldn't even use them as examples.

The practice of customer satisfaction is not limited to how you treat customers *after* you acquire them; it should also focus on what you do to attain them in the first place. The quality of the clients you attain will have a direct effect on your level of customer satisfaction. You will not get to quality without seeking quantity. Remember as well what we discussed in the previous chapter: that criticisms and complaints are inevitable indications that you are growing as you should. So disregard criticism, welcome and handle complaints, and do everything you can to expand your footprint. The more people you serve, the better your chances are of interacting with quality customers.

To be clear, you certainly want to deliver—and exceed— on the promises you make. However, if you focus on delivering exceptional 10X service prior to acquisition, this part will come naturally after acquisition. I am assuming you have a great product, service, idea, or investment. Now you need to increase your support base for it. There are, regrettably, thousands of organizations in existence that sell inferior products every day. Although I'm certainly not suggesting you push substandard offerings or sacrifice your product's quality, I am trying to highlight an unfortunate reality: Domination of market share tends to trump all other things. Companies that sell poor products make acquisitions their number one goal— and then handle any problems with their products or offerings after they get users on board.

No organization in the world has created massive success while limiting its acquisitions. Apple learned this lesson the hard way for too long. It got killed by Microsoft for decades—a company any Apple user will claim sold an inferior product—because while Microsoft made its merchandise available to the masses, Apple focused on just a small number of people. Notice the shift that Apple has made in the past few years, making its products appealing to the masses. Three percent of all households have an iPad, and 63 percent are using an MP3 player, with Apple getting over 45 percent of that share. Apple is clearly adopting "massive action" in a big way these days with the goal of dominating with its footprint!

Remember, even if your product and company deliver perfectly, you are going to get complaints from customers—because they're human. You can't keep everyone happy all the time. It's a mistake to be scared of complaints. Instead, encourage them, look for them, find them, and then resolve them. Complaints are your customers' very direct way of telling you exactly how to make your product better. If you approach every situation wrought with anxiety about offending a client, then you will never attain dominance in the market.

Let's go back to Apple as an example. This company doesn't worry today about customer satisfaction so much that it neglects to continue building products that people are willing to stand in line to get. It recognizes the proper order of objectives: (1) acquire customers (via an amazing product or service that you've worked on at 10X levels to create); (2) impress them with how great you are during the acquisition process; and (3) establish customer loyalty (through repeat purchases, support, word-of-mouth marketing, etc.). When you're building a business, your primary target is not customer satisfaction (yet); it's acquisition, referral, and loyalty and then *more* acquisition using the customers you've attained. I want everyone to have my products, not just some people. I want masses of people—not just a few—to know about me and my products. I won't be satisfied until 6 billion people do. I want everyone to purchase from me over and over, and I want to be on their minds so regularly—and make such an impact on them and their companies—that they never even think about using anyone else.

This line of thinking differs from concentrating so intensely on customer satisfaction that members of the sales team worry about upsetting, pressuring, and pressing hard for fear that doing so may damage their clients' opinion of them. I know sales teams that are penalized when they receive customer complaints, which seems odd to me for several reasons. For one, it suggests that these grievances could be avoided, which they clearly cannot. Even if you could avoid them, why would you want to? Complaints and problems are opportunities to do more business and solve more issues—and to give your customers the chance to spread the word about how great you are at making their problems go away!

If you truly want to find out what your organization's customer acquisition and loyalty weaknesses are, then survey the people who you do *not* acquire. The sooner you can ask them questions, the better—ideally, as they leave or refuse the business. And be sure to ask them about the *processes*—not about the people—they encountered. You might ask questions like the following:

How long were you here?

Did you meet a manager?

Were you shown optional products?

Were you presented with a proposal?

Did anyone offer to bring the product to your home/office?

Feel free to call my office for guidance on how to develop this survey for your unique situation (800-368-5771). We can help identify what to ask in order to pinpoint where the breakdown is taking place.

When was the last time you were asked to give a company that you decided *not* to purchase from your feedback on the experience? Did the salespeople give you enough attention? Did they stay with you through your decision-making process? Did they meet you enthusiastically, offer to solve your problems, have someone from management say hello, show you various options—or even present their product or a proposal? And did anyone call you back? I bet the answer to most of these questions is no. *Companies fail not because they offend customers but because they don't take enough action to make these individuals customers in the first place.* And I assure you that these very same companies hold one meeting after another on improving customer satisfaction. They will survey those who buy from them instead of taking the time to ask those who didn't why. Add to this the fact that most of these surveys focus on what the sales associate did wrong rather than on what is inadequate about the organization's thinking and processes.

Remember the operative order of importance: customer acquisition is the primary target, followed by customer loyalty, followed by customers who spread the word about you. This approach allows a company to continue to invest in product development and improvement, enhance processes, and increase promotion—which ultimately creates *real* customer satisfaction.

Exercise

Have you ever been surveyed by a company that you didn't buy from?

_____

_____

_____

What is more important than customer satisfaction?

1. _____

_____

_____

_____

2. _____

_____

_____

_____

Why do most businesses fail?

_____

_____

_____

_____

What might be some survey questions you could use when you don't acquire a customer?

_____

_____

_____

_____

CHAPTER
20

Omnipresence

The word "omnipresence" conveys the concept of being everywhere—in all places, at all times. Can you imagine what it would be like if you, your brand, and your company could be everywhere all the time—and how much power this would give you? Although it may seem impossible, this should be your goal. The things that are assigned the most value on this planet are believed to be available everywhere. It is impossible to amass true success without thinking in terms of making your ideas, products, services, or brand universal. The things upon which people depend most are omnipresent, from the oxygen you breathe to the water you drink to the fuel you burn in your car to the electricity that runs through your home to the most impressively branded products on earth. What these items have in common is that they're accessible everywhere. You see them, constantly, depend on them, and have become used to needing them, in most cases, on a daily basis.

Consider something as seemingly obvious as the news. TV channels, newspapers, radio, and the Internet deliver the news 24/7—so that's usually what's on people's minds most frequently. We see it when we wake up, we talk about it at the water cooler, we hear about it throughout the day, and we watch it on television before we go to sleep.

This is the kind of mind-set from which you must operate—to make yourself available everywhere. You want people to see you so often that they think of you constantly and instantaneously identify your face or name or logo with not just the offering you represent but even the offering made by those similar to you. Many people incorrectly assume that they can make a handful of phone calls, a personal visit or two, and send out some e-mails and somehow command people's attention. But the truth is that none of these actions will cause people to think about you enough to have a considerable effect. Are you operating at the right level of targeting, and thinking big enough? If you're not already, you need to expand your approach and enlarge your footprint with the goal of dominating and being everywhere.

My goal these days is to get more than 6 billion people to hear my name constantly, know it when they hear it, and then when they think sales training, they think of me. Although this may seem unrealistic, probably unattainable, it is the right target, thinking, footprint, and concept for my business—to be everywhere. The mere commitment to doing something this big will be an adventure in and of itself. Even before I'm able to fully attain my goal, I will achieve some greater level of success in the attempt. Will money come as a result? Absolutely! Will people buy my products? For sure! Will I create success for my ideas and get support for whatever I am trying to accomplish? Guaranteed!

This mind-set will then allow for us to make all our decisions with the goal of moving me in the direction of getting everyone on the planet to know about me, my products, my company, and my efforts! Every decision we make at my company is based on this one mission: Introduce the entire planet to Grant Cardone. Although our targets have to be funded, money is not our primary interest. We know profits will come as a result of our efforts to be everywhere at the same time. We don't ask what a project will cost or whether it fits in the budget or if we have time to do something. We ask, does it help us accomplish the mission of being everywhere? We don't stop to figure out whether I want to travel or speak to a smaller group or what the outcome may be. We simply do not allow any excuses and distractions that could limit expansion. In the same way, any attempt you make to have yourself, your brand, your product, or your service be omnipresent will automatically guide your actions and decisions.

Is this kind of thinking too big? For most people, it is. Is it absolutely necessary? Well, not if you are willing to settle for average. However, if you are considering that, go back and reread the chapters on why average goals will fail you and why normal does not work. Show me one great company that has not accomplished omnipresence. Coca-Cola, McDonald's, Google, Starbucks, Phillip Morris, AT&T, La-Z-Boy, Bank of America, World Disney, Fox TV, Apple, Ernst & Young, Ford Motor Company, Visa, American Express, Macy's, Wal-Mart, Best Buy—these names are everywhere. Each of these companies is in every city—some on every street corner—and most are available around the world. You see their ads, you know what their logos look like, and you can even hum some of their jingles and use their names to describe not just their products; but in some cases, their competitors' products as well.

There are also individuals who have accomplished omnipresence so well that the world immediately recognizes their names, such as Oprah, Bill Gates, Warren Buffett, George Bush, Barack Obama, Abe Lincoln, Elvis, the Beatles, Led Zeppelin, Walt Disney, Will Smith, Mother Teresa, Muhammad Ali, Michael Jackson, Michael Jordan, and so on. Whether you like them or not, each of these people has created such a name for himself or herself that most people *know* who they are—or at the very least, recognize their name and align it with importance. The way in which they manage and control their brands will determine their long-term success and survivability.

My father always gave me the following valuable advice: "Your name is your most important asset. [People] can take everything away from you—but they can't take your name." Although I agree with my dad's emphasis on the importance of names, it of course becomes less important if no one knows it. Unless people know who you are, no one will pay attention to what you represent. You have to get people to know you, which means that you have to get attention. The more attention you get, the more places you will be; the more people you are with, the more you can be everywhere. And all of this will improve your chances of using your good name to do good work.

Have you ever heard the saying, "It is enough if you can just help one person"? Although it's surely a good thing to help one person—and certainly better than helping no one—I personally don't really believe helping just one person is enough. I know it sounds good and that this saying emphasizes the importance of helping others, but there are 6.8 billion people on this planet, and most of them need *some* kind of help. Your goal must—and can—be bigger than "just one person." And in order for this to happen, people must know who you are and what you represent! Otherwise, you will not be able to help even one person—much less make a dent in 6.8 billion.

You must think in terms of being everywhere at all times. This is the kind of 10X mind-set necessary to dominate your sector. If you commit to taking 10X actions consistently, followed up with more 10X actions, then I assure you that you will be propelled into situations where you *find* yourself everywhere. The first thing you have to do is burst through obscurity and let the world know what you can do for it—and then do it relentlessly. Although it might sound like a grind, it will only be a chore if your goals are too small, self-serving—and unattained. I promise it won't feel like a grind when you come out on top. You may want to get rich—but why? What do you want to use the money for? Do you have a higher purpose you're looking to serve? After all, you can only accumulate so much personal wealth before it doesn't matter anymore. Maybe you want to amass riches in order to help more people and improve conditions for all mankind. That would require you to be omnipresent—everywhere, all the time.

The higher your purpose, the more fuel it will provide for your 10X actions. This is what it takes to rocket to omnipresence. People of fame and influence achieve this status because they are compelled to fulfill their purpose by writing books, doing interviews, blogging, writing articles, accepting speaking engagements, and saying yes constantly to get attention for themselves, their companies, and their projects. These are the results of thinking big. This isn't a grind; this is passion. It is only a grind when your mind-set and actions are too small and will not create enough of a payoff. You are capable of much more than you're doing now. Once you match your mind-set with the right purpose, you will start taking 10X actions—and find yourself simultaneously propelled into more places than you ever thought possible.

In order for your life not to feel like "work" or like you're running on a hamster wheel—you must think in terms of the right volumes. Omnipresence—the goal of being everywhere at all times and at the same time—is exactly the kind of massive thinking that is missing from most people's expectations of themselves and their dreams.

You must first make a vow to have your brand, idea, concept, company, product, or service make a footprint on the planet. To do so, you have to get involved with your community, school system, neighborhood, and local politics. You have to attend and be seen at events, write in the local paper, and get connected to the players in your community. Once involved do everything possible to stay active, have people see you, read you, hear you, and think about you. Say yes to every opportunity to get your word out. Write about it, talk about it, give lectures on what you do, and even bark on the street corners if you have to. Commit to omnipresence!

I didn't learn this incredibly important lesson myself until I was under major attack by people who didn't want to see me doing well and I had to figure out how to counter it. My gut reaction was to retaliate immediately by way of inflicting physical harm (which I felt in a fleeting moment of insanity). However, my wife reminded me of my own saying: "The best revenge is massive success." She advised me to move forward with such great momentum and so much of a presence that every time these people woke up, turned the TV on, or made a business move, they would see my face—and be reminded of how well I was doing. Hearing the truth from my sane and positive wife immediately put me at ease—and made it clear to me that the best payback possible was not force of any kind but simply amassing more success.

Rather than spending energy on retaliating, I spent all my energy, resources, and creativity on becoming omnipresent and expanding my footprint. This is a much better investment in energy than chasing someone else down. Consider how you can use this illustration to figure out how you can be in more places at the same time. Immediately after this attack, I got very busy making sure I was seen everywhere all the time. I wrote my first book and followed it up with another one three months later. I then finished my third book, and members of my group spent months doing everything possible to make it a *New York Times* best-seller—which they did!

The goal was to do everything we could to get my information and material disseminated. We started using YouTube and Flickr to provide motivational videos, sales tips, and business strategies to our clients—and asked people to pass them on to their friends. I personally recorded more than 200 videos, wrote 150 blogs and articles, and did 700 radio interviews in 18 months. I then began getting national TV exposure with the networks and cable TV. Fox, CNBC, MSNBC, CNN radio, WSJ radio, and more all started having me on their shows. In the same period, I personally wrote more than 2,000 posts on Facebook, Twitter, and LinkedIn. All of this was in addition to what my office was diligently doing to get my name out. My face, name, voice, articles, methodologies, and videos began showing up everywhere—many at the same time. People with whom I had never done business started saying to us, "I see your name everywhere!" I was completely focused on expanding my footprint and making myself known to the rest of the world rather than worrying about a small group of critics.

My business blew up on every front. Opportunities started to flow in daily. We started getting attention not just from those we had been focused on but from people all over the world. As a result of this campaign, my books are being translated into Chinese and German. Now inquires from France, Mexico, South Africa, and other countries are flowing in with interest in our sales training programs and books. We have people calling us from both here in the United States and overseas who are interested in TV programs and doing magazine articles. I am not bragging here but showing you what can happen for you when you take the right actions at the right levels and start thinking in the right size.

All powerful companies, ideas, products, and people are omnipresent. They can be found everywhere. They dominate their sector and become synonymous with that which they represent. Real success is measured by longevity. So if you want to be excited and passionate for the long haul, then make omnipresence your constant goal. Your name, brand, and reputation are your most valuable assets only if enough people know of them and use them. And remember, *the best way to even the score against those who have it in for you is to make yourself so well known that every time they look up—each morning when they wake and right before they go to sleep at night—they see evidence of you and your success.*

Exercise

What does it mean to be *omnipresent*?

_____

_____

_____

_____

_____

What steps do you need to take to become omnipresent?

_____

_____

_____

_____

_____

What is the upside of taking so much action that the marketplace makes your name synonymous with what it is you represent?

_____

_____

_____

_____

_____

What is the best way to get revenge against your critics?

_____

_____

_____

_____

_____

CHAPTER

21

Excuses

This is about the time we should look at the excuses you are likely going to use to avoid making any of this happen. Everyone uses excuses. Most people actually have favorites that they employ over and over. I am certain that yours are starting to emerge by now—so rather than ignore them, let's just go ahead and confront the little monsters so that they don't distract you later.

An "excuse" is a justification for doing—or not doing—something. I think the dictionary implies that it's a "reason." However, in reality, an excuse usually turns out to be something *other* than the real reason that motivates your actions (or lack thereof). For example, let's say that your excuse for being late to work is due to traffic. Well, that's not truly the *reason* you didn't make it to work on time. The reason you were late is because you left your home without enough time to allow for traffic. *Excuses are never the reason for why you did or didn't do something. They're just a revision of the facts that you make up in order to help yourself feel better about what happened (or didn't)*. Making excuses won't change your situation; only getting to the real reason behind it can do this. Excuses are for people who refuse to take responsibility for their life and how it turns out. Slaves and victims make excuses—and will forever be destined to having leftovers and others' scraps.

The first thing to know about excuses is that they never improve your situation. The second thing to know is which ones you use on a regular basis. Do any of the following sound familiar? I don't have the money, I have kids, I don't have kids, I am married, I am not married, I have to find balance in my life, I am overworked, I am underworked, too many people work here, we don't have enough people, my manager sucks/doesn't help me/won't leave me alone/is negative/is too jacked up, I don't like reading, I don't have time to study, I don't have time for anything, our prices are too high, our prices are too low, the customer won't call me back, the customer cancelled the appointment, people don't tell me the truth, they don't have the money, the economy is bad, the banks aren't lending, my owner is cheap, we don't have/can't find the right people, no one is motivated, people have bad attitudes, no one told me, it was someone else's fault, they keep changing their minds, I am tired, I need a vacation, the people I work with are losers, I'm depressed, I'm sick, my mom is sick, traffic is terrible, the competition is giving its product away, I have such bad luck. . . .

Bored yet? I know I am! I had to really reach deep into the recesses of my mind just to come up with some of those. How many of these have you used? Go back and circle every statement you've *ever* heard come out of your mouth. Now ask yourself, will any of these excuses ever improve your condition? I doubt it.

So why, then, do so many people make them so often? Does it even matter? An excuse is just an alteration of reality; nothing about it will move you to a better situation. The fact that "the customer doesn't have the money" will not help you close your deal. The fact that you "only have bad luck" is not going to improve the conditions of your life or change your luck. In fact, if you keep telling yourself that long enough, you'll start to expect it—thereby *ensuring* that things will continue to be bad.

You have to start understanding the differences between making excuses and providing actual, sound reasons for events. This book focuses on the many differences between the successful and the unsuccessful—and a very distinct dissimilarity is that successful people simply don't make excuses. They are actually quite unreasonable when it comes to providing reasons—at least for failure—as well. I'll never ask myself (or anyone else, for that matter) why I was unable to bring my product to market, raise enough money, or make enough sales because as far as I'm concerned, no answer will do. There are no justifications that will change these facts or situations—and any reasons I might provide are only opportunities yet to be handled. Any rationale you give yourself just gives someone else the chance to find a solution. Remember what I've said time and again throughout this book: "Nothing happens *to* you; it happens *because* of you." Excuses are just another component of this—and a major differentiator between whether you will succeed or not.

If you make success an option, then it won't be an option for you—simple. No excuse exists that can or will make you successful. Engaging in self-pity and excuse making are signs that someone has an extremely minimal degree of responsibility. "He didn't buy from me because the bank wouldn't make the loan." No, he didn't buy from you because you were unable to secure proper financing for a potential customer. The first statement assumes no responsibility for the event, while the other does—and identifies a solution. Once you adopt a more advanced sense of responsibility—and refuse to make any more excuses—then you can go out and search for a solution. And as an added bonus, you will avoid such situations in the future.

The quality of being rare is what makes something valuable. So anything that is plentiful has very little worth. Excuses are one item that people seem to have an almost endless supply of. Because they are so plentiful, they have no value. Because they do not forward your desire to create more success for yourself, they are worthless uses of your energy. If you are going to approach success as you've been taught throughout this book—not as an option but as your duty, obligation, and responsibility—then you must commit to *never* using excuses for *anything*! You cannot allow yourself, your team, your family, or anyone in your organization to use another excuse as a reason why something didn't come to fruition. As the old saying goes, "If it is to be, it is up to me."

Exercise

What is the difference between an excuse and a reason?

_____

_____

_____

_____

_____

What are the two things you know about excuses?

_____

_____

_____

_____

_____

What excuses have you been using?

_____

_____

_____

_____

22

Successful or Unsuccessful?

I have been studying successful people most of my life and have found the differences between them and the people who accomplish less worth noting—and its not what you might expect. The distinctions between these two groups have nothing to do with economics, education, or demographics. Although these experiences and events certainly influenced them and their viewpoints, they are not ultimately the determining factors in their lives. I can show you people with no education, who were reared by broken families in terrible surroundings, but still managed to grow their successes to stratospheric levels.

Successful people talk, think, and approach situations, challenges, and problems differently than most people—and they definitely think about money differently. Listed in this chapter are the commonly found qualities, personality traits, and habits that make successful people the way they are. Each item is followed by a few of my thoughts on what each category means. This will allow you to become more aware of the kinds of habits and characteristics you should be developing—and encouraging your employees and colleagues to develop as well. The only way to be successful is to take the same actions that successful people take. Success is no different than any other skill. Duplicate the actions and mind-sets of successful people, and you will create success for yourself.

The following list of ways you should act in order to be successful is based on what I have discovered about successful people and the way they do things.

1. Have a "Can Do" Attitude

People with a "can do" attitude approach every situation with the outlook that no matter what, it can be done. They consistently use phrases like "We can do it," "Let's make it happen," "Let's work it out"—and they always maintain that a solution exists. These people talk in terms of explanations and resolving issues and consistently communicate challenges with a positive outlook. They respond to even the most daunting or seemingly impossible situation in a "can do" manner. This attitude is more valuable than a superior product and a lower price and is one of the only ways you'll be able to accomplish 10X massive actions. If you are not willing to approach everything with the attitude that it can be done, then you won't truly be thinking in 10X. You must believe and convey to others that a solution does indeed exist—even if you're going to have to work a little harder to find it. Incorporate this kind of "can do" outlook into your language, thoughts, actions, and responses to everyone you know. Help your entire company develop this kind of attitude by drilling it into them on a daily basis. Take even the most impossible request and figure out how you can answer with a "can do" attitude. Get yourself and your colleagues to the point where responses like "Can do, no problem—we will handle it!" become the norm—and nothing else is even accepted.

2. Believe That "I Will Figure It Out"

This outlook goes hand in hand with the "can do" attitude. Again, it refers to the individual who is always looking to be responsible and solve a problem. Even if you're not sure how to do something, the best answer is "I will figure it out"—not "I don't know." No one values a person who not only doesn't have the information but doesn't *want* to know the information. This response does nothing for your credibility or competence. I don't agree with the claim that you should tell people if you don't know something. How does this help the situation? Do you really want to brag about your inability or think that the marketplace—or your customers—value honesty *so* much that they want you to admit they are wasting their time with you? You can admit that you're unfamiliar with something—as long as you immediately follow that admission up with the promise that you will figure it out or find someone who will. Throwing up your hands at a task will not move things forward. Communicate to yourself and others that you are *willing* to do what is necessary to figure it out! An alternative response to "I don't know" is "Great question. Let me check into that and figure it out." You are still being honest, but you're inciting a solution instead of implying ineptitude.

3. Focus on Opportunity

Successful people see all situations—even problems and complaints—as opportunities. Where others see difficulty, successful individuals know that problems solved equal new products, services, customers—and probably financial success. Remember: Success is overcoming a challenge. Therefore, you can't succeed *without* some kind of difficulty. It doesn't really matter what the challenge is; as long as you handle it adequately, you'll be rewarded. And the bigger the problem is, the bigger the opportunity as well. When a problem exists for the entire market and all the people in it, it becomes an equalizer. The only person who stands out is the opportunity-focused individual who sees those problems as openings for success. These people are able to use the issue at hand to separate themselves and dominate the marketplace. There are countless situations that most people tend to see as setbacks and nothing else: recessions, unemployment, housing predicaments, conflict, customer complaints, and company shutdowns, to name a few. If you can learn to see these as prospects instead of problems, you'll continually come out on top.

4. Love Challenges

Whereas many people loathe challenges—and use them as reasons to sink further into indifference—highly successful individuals are compelled and invigorated by challenges. The idea of being overwhelmed, I believe, is the result of never taking enough action to generate enough winning. Success begets more success, and losses increase your chances of more losses. Challenges are the experiences that sharpen successful people's abilities. To achieve your goals, you have to get to a place where every challenge becomes fuel for you. Life can be quite brutal, and people can incur a fair amount of losses over time. Many get to a point where every new challenge they face automatically equals a loss in their mind. There are ways to rehabilitate yourself, however, so that the hardships you've experienced throughout your life no longer rob you of the chance to approach new challenges with gusto and excitement.

When you are able to develop a more positive outlook, you begin to see a challenge as stimulation to engage—rather than as an excuse to avoid something. You have to reeducate yourself on the notion of this thing called a "challenge"—and know that every challenge provides an opportunity to win. And don't kid yourself—winning in life is vital. Every minute of every day, your mind is automatically keeping a running tab on your wins, losses, and ties—and is doing so based on what you know to be your full potential. The more you win in life, the higher your potential will be—and the more you will grow to love challenges.

5. Seek to Solve Problems

Successful individuals love to seek out problems because they know that almost every problem is universal in some way or another. Some industries actually *create* problems so that they can "solve" them by way of selling their products to you. (Think of all the things you've purchased over the years because you "needed" them. Did you really? Or were you convinced that they would solve some problem you may or may not have had?) Flu shots are a great example. Many people think they are necessary, but medical opinion is divided on this matter. Problems for the successful are like a meal to the hungry. Give me a problem—any problem—and when I solve it, I will be rewarded and I may become a hero. The bigger the problems—and the more people who benefit from the solution—the more powerful your success will be. You get yourself on the successful list by seeking problems to solve—for your company, employees, customers, the government—whatever they may be and wherever they might exist. The world is filled with people who have—and who unfortunately, cause—problems. One of the fastest and best ways to separate yourself from the masses is to establish yourself as someone who makes situations better, not worse.

6. Persist until Successful

The ability to persist on a given path regardless of setbacks, unexpected events, bad news, and resistance—to continue steadfastly or firmly in some state, purpose, or course of action in spite of conditions—is a trait common to those who make it. I assure you that I, at least, am more persistent than I am talented. This isn't a trait that people do or do not have; it's something that can—and must—be developed. Children seem to display this quality innately until they come to see—via socialization, parenting, or a combination of both—that it's not how most people act. However, this quality is necessary to make any dream a reality.

Whether you are a salesperson or state person, employer or employee, you will have to learn how to persist through all types of situations. It is as though this planet has some kind of force or natural tendency—almost like gravity—that challenges people's ability to persist. It's almost like the universe is just trying to find out what you are made of as it continues to confront you. I know that any endeavor I tackle will require me to persist with 10X actions until all resistance morphs into support. I don't try to eliminate resistance; I merely keep going until the course changes and my ideas are maintained instead of defied. For example, I had a heckler on Facebook whose support I tried to gain but couldn't. Rather than deleting that person, I asked my followers on Facebook what they thought of the situation and let them bury the guy and further support me. If something doesn't end up supporting me, I simply persist with so much success that any remaining resistance will cease to exist.

Persistence is a great advantage to anyone who wants to multiply his or her success—because most other people have given up on their innate ability to persist. When you retrain yourself to do whatever is necessary to ensure that you are in the best mental, emotional, and financial position to persevere— you will find yourself on the list of the most successful.

7. Take Risks

Once when I was in Vegas, a man sitting next to me said, "These casinos will always make money because the people that play here are never willing to take risks at levels great enough to wipe them out." I am not suggesting that you go out and try to take a casino down; however, the man's observation reminded me of how many of us are taught to play it safe, be conservative, and never really "go for it" in a big way. Life is not a great deal different than Vegas; you must put something into the game in order to get a return. At some point, you will *have* to take a risk, and the successful are willing to do so daily. In the truly big casinos of life and business, do you really take enough risk to create the success you want and need? Most people never go far enough in getting recognized, gaining attention, and making a big splash; they are trying to protect or conserve a reputation, a position, or some already achieved state. The successful are willing to take gambles—to put it all out there and know, regardless of the outcome, that they can go back and do it again. They allow themselves to be criticized, looked at, and seen by the world—while the unsuccessful hold back and play it safe. Remember the old saying, "Nothing ventured, nothing gained." At this time, it is vital that you get your family and friends to be supportive of you in taking risks and in no longer playing it safe.

8. Be Unreasonable

No, that is not an error; it does say *un*reasonable. In my book *Sell to Survive*, I introduced the notion that the successful salesperson must be unreasonable with his or her client in order to consummate the sale. This clearly flies in the face of what most of us are taught—that is, to be reasonable and logical. Being unreasonable requires that you act without rational consideration and not in accordance with practical realities.

And, yes—that's what I want you to do! When most people see this definition, they get confused and think that I'm telling them to be crazy. But successful people recognize how vital it is to act without reason. They know they cannot afford to act in accordance with the agreed-upon realities. If they do, the supposed "impossible" can never become possible for them. Being a 10X-er requires thinking and acting unreasonably. Otherwise, you will end up the same way everyone else does—forced to survive on successful people's leftovers. Unreasonable doesn't mean being mentally unstable—and let's face it, who isn't just a little off the rocker—but that you refuse to validate the alleged "sanity" of reasonable actions that will never get you what you want. Most of the world is playing in accordance with some set of stupid, useless, reasonable rules that only ensure that you continue trudging along in bondage as a mere slave. Think about it: Would we have cars, airplanes, space travel, telephones, and the Internet—in addition to thousands of other things we take for granted—if someone hadn't done something that another person had labeled "unreasonable"? Man would do nothing exceptional if it were not for the willingness to be unreasonable. So be one of the unreasonable ones. They are usually the people who make a huge difference in our world.

9. Be Dangerous

Since you were a child, someone has been trying to keep you from danger. "Be careful" is the mantra that parents repeat to their children while buying products from entire industries that have been created just to "safe proof" a home in order to protect a child. Unfortunately, many people get to the point where they're so intent upon avoiding danger that they cease to truly live life! If you look back over your life, you'll probably see that you have done yourself just as much—or even more—harm by being "careful" than by being dangerous.

Think about the last time you got hurt. You were probably trying to protect something right before it happened. Being careful requires you to take actions cautiously—and there is no way that you will *ever* hit 10X activity levels by being cautious. Massive action demands that you throw caution to the wind, even if it puts you in the path of danger. Working with powerful people is dangerous in and of itself. Do you want to get investment dollars from a billionaire? A salary that pays you a million dollars a year? Take your company public? If so, you have to be willing to be dangerous because more will be expected of you with each of those situations. To do something big, you have to embrace danger. The way to ensure that danger doesn't kill you is to be sufficiently trained so that you can get into the ring and come out the victor.

10. Create Wealth

Attitude toward wealth is an especially significant distinction between the financially successful and the unsuccessful. Poor people believe they need to work in order to make money and then spend their lives either spending it on nothing of importance or conserving like crazy in order to protect it. The very successful know that the money is already created. They think in terms of generating wealth through the exchange of new ideas, products, services, and solutions. The very successful realize that they're not bound by shortages. They know that money exists in abundance and flows to those who create products, services, and solutions—and that wealth is not limited to a monetary supply. The closer you are to the massive flows of money, the better chance you have of creating wealth for your own endeavors.

Think in terms of creating money and wealth, not salaries and conservation of funds. Figure out how to create wealth through the exchange of great ideas, quality service, and effective problem solving. Look, for example, at how powerful banks behave. They collect currency through methods that compel other people to either give them money or borrow it from them. Consider the way in which wealthy people own real estate that others pay for by way of rent. They produce money solely by owning this property and therefore create wealth. People who invest in their own companies do so in order to increase their wealth, not their incomes. The unsuccessful, on the other hand, spend money on things that affluent individuals use to create wealth. Income is taxed; wealth is not. Remember: You don't need to "make" money. It has already been made. There are no shortages of actual money—only shortages of people creating wealth. Move your attention from conserving money to creating wealth, and you'll be thinking as successful people do.

11. Readily Take Action

This is entirely what this book is about (I hope that much is clear by now!). The highly successful take unbelievable amounts of action. Regardless of what that action looks like, these people rarely do nothing—even when they are on vacation (just ask their spouses or families!). Whether it is by way of getting others to take action for them, getting attention for their products or ideas, or just grinding it out day and night, the successful have been consistently taking high levels of action— before anyone ever heard their names. The unsuccessful talk about a plan for action but never quite get around to doing what they claim they're going to do—at least enough to ever get what they want. Successful people assume that their future achievements rely on investing in actions that may not pay off today but that when taken consistently and persistently over time will sooner or later bear fruit.

Massive action is the one thing I know I can depend on from myself, even when times are tough. Your ability to take action will be a major factor in determining your potential success—and is a discipline that you should spend time on daily. It's not a gift or trait I was "lucky" enough to receive or inherit; it's a habit that must be developed. Laziness and lack of action are ethical issues for me. I don't think it's right or acceptable for me to be lazy. It is not a "character flaw" that's caused by some invented disease, any more than a highly active person is somehow "blessed." No one is born to sprint or run a marathon any more than some people are born to take more action than others. Action is necessary in order to create success and can be the single defining quality that will enable you to make the list of successful people. No matter who you are or what you've done in life so far, you *can* develop this habit in order to enhance your success.

12. Always Say "Yes"

To really go at it in life and in business, you have to say yes to everything. It's something you'll see successful people do time and again—not because they can but because they *choose* to say yes. They eagerly engage in life and realize that the word "yes" has more life and possibilities in it—and is clearly so much more positive than "no." When a client asks me to do something, I say, "Yes, I will be happy to/would love to/want to make it work for you." I have a saying: "I never say no until I have to." It's a great way to tell someone no (that is, if you *absolutely* must). When given an option to do or not do something, always say yes! Life is to be lived—something that becomes impossible to do when you're constantly saying no. Although many suggest that it is critical to know what to say no to, the reality is most people don't venture out and don't experience enough in life. They refuse to take on new things and experiences as often as they should. You know that you have an automatic "no" in you all ready to go—one that is backed with a 100 reasons why you can't, shouldn't, or don't have time to do something. Give this a try: Say yes for now until you become so successful that you are forced to add "no" to your arsenal and start managing your time and efforts. Until then, make "yes" part of your successful habits. Say yes to your kids, spouse, clients, boss, and most importantly, to yourself. It will propel you to new adventures, new solutions, and new levels of success.

13. Habitually Commit

The successful fully and consistently commit to activities—some of which require them to put it all on the line. This goes back to the concept of being "all in" that I described earlier. It also relates to operating with some level of danger and refusing to play it safe. Unsuccessful people rarely commit to anything entirely. They are always talking about "trying," and when they do commit, it is normally in destructive acts and habits. Commitment is actually one of the things of which there *is* a shortage. Far too many individuals and organizations fail to commit fully to their activities, duties, obligations, and responsibilities to see things all the way through. To acquire success, it is vital that you quit testing the water's temperature and simply jump in! Devoting yourself to something all the way means that there's no backing out. It is just like when you jump into a body of water; once you decide to go for it, you can't stop yourself midair.

I would prefer a person who is able to fully commit over one who is completely educated any day. Commitment is a sign that someone is pledging him- or herself completely to a position, issue, or action. Successful people see past the problems and are able to keep their focus on the promise they've made to themselves or others. They keep their eyes on the outcome or action the entire time. When I commit to ensuring success for myself, my family, a project, or my company, it means that I will do whatever is necessary to make that pledge a reality and fulfill my commitment. Commitments are not something for which you can make excuses, nor are they something you negotiate with or on which you can "give up." Commit fully as though you are already successful and demonstrate that commitment to all those with—and for—whom you work.

14. Go All the Way

As they say in AA, "Half measures achieved us nothing." For members, this means that you can't get sober if you are drinking—even a little bit. In the world of success and achievements, half measures achieve nothing in terms of results—except for tiring out the person engaging in the half measures. This is why most people refer to work as though it were an illness. Only those who go all the way and see things through until they're done experience the rewards that the workplace has to offer. Until an action is turned into a success, it is not done. Until you make the potential client a client or the potential investor an investor, you have not gone all the way. This might seem harsh, but if you called a client 50 times and didn't get the deal done, then you might as well have not called that person at all. This is the point at which people become reasonable and therefore don't make it. Commit to being completely unreasonable and going all the way. Don't accept any excuses! No settling allowed!

15. Focus on "Now"

There exist only two times for the successful: now and the future. The unsuccessful spend most of their time in the past and regard the future as an opportunity to procrastinate. "Now" is the period of time that successful people utilize most often to create the futures they desire in order to dominate their environments. You cannot do what unsuccessful people do, which is to use any excuse they can think of to put off the tasks they should be completing immediately. Instead, you must acquire the discipline, muscle memory, and achievements that result from taking massive action—while others think, plan, and procrastinate. Taking actions immediately allows the most successful to design the future they desire. The successful understand that they must keep taking actions now. They're well aware that procrastination is the ultimate weakness.

The 10X Rule requires that you take action in massive quantities and immediately. Anyone who puts off doing what he or she can do right now will never gain the momentum and confidence that result from doing so. For example, I once told my staff that I wanted each one of them—even those in administrative positions—to make 50 phone calls. I immediately saw signs of panic appear on everyone's face—as though this would be impossible to achieve, what with everything else they had to do. So I told them, "You each have 30 minutes to make your calls—go!" I then went to my office and made 28 phone calls in 22 minutes.

You cannot allow even one second of worry or analysis to delay you in situations like these—because every second you spend thinking is a second of action that you're wasting! You will be amazed how much you can get done when you quit thinking, calculating, and procrastinating and just get on with it and make a habit of acting now. Although this may cause you to feel like you are reacting constantly—causing you to be too spontaneous—it will also make acting a habit. Action is necessary—and there is no time more valuable than now. While others are trying to figure out how they will get something done, you will have already finished it. The person who continues to *do* more consistently will improve his or her skill set out of sheer survival and adjustment. Discipline yourself to perform now—not later—and I assure you that the volume of endeavors you are undertaking will quickly increase the quality of work—and propel you to move with enhanced conviction and certainty.

16. Demonstrate Courage

Courage is that quality of mind or spirit that compels people to face dangerous situations in spite of fear. It's rare that people feel or are described as courageous before the event that compels them to act in this way. Rather, they're referred to as such as a result of taking action regardless of their fears. Soldiers and heroes never refer to themselves as brave before they endure hardships. As far as they're concerned, they're just doing what they have to do at that moment.

You'll often notice that successful people carry themselves with an air of confidence and conviction, a sense of comfort, and maybe even a touch of arrogance. Before you start thinking that they are somehow inherently "different," you should understand that they acquired these qualities as a result of taking action. The more frequently you can do things that scare you a bit, the more others will label you as courageous—and then gravitate toward you. Courage comes to those who act, not to those who think, wait, and wonder. The only way to hone this trait is by taking action. Although you can train to increase your skills and your confidence, courage is only attained by *doing*—especially doing things that you fear. Who wants to do business with or support someone who readily gives in to his or her fears? Who wants to invest in a project when the people behind it don't act with confidence and courage?

I was recently interviewed by someone who asked me, "Does *nothing* scare you?" The question surprised me because I know that I experience fear. I suppose that it must appear that I am not scared because I deliver fourth degree actions—and you can certainly do the same. Attack, dominate, and keep your attention on the future, and then continue to repeat your actions—and your courage will grow. Do things that scare you more frequently, and they will slowly begin to scare you a bit less—until they become so habitual that you wonder why you ever feared them in the first place!

17. Embrace Change

Successful people love change, whereas the unsuccessful do everything they can to keep things from changing. But how can you create success when you are trying to keep things from becoming any different? It is impossible. Although you never want to alter the things that are working, you should always look for ways to improve what you are doing. The successful keep an eye out for what is coming next. They seek out potential, upcoming market transformations and embrace them instead of rejecting them. The successful look at how the world is shifting and apply this to how they might improve their operations and grow their advantage. They never subsist on yesterday's successes. They know that they must continue to adapt or they won't remain victorious. Change is not something to resist; it's something that should keep you excited. Apple's Steve Jobs is a great example of this. He changes his products before a competitor can catch up or his consumers can get bored with them. The willingness to accept change is a great quality of the successful.

18. Determine and Take the Right Approach

The successful know that they can quantify what works and what doesn't work, whereas the unsuccessful focus solely on "hard work." The right approach may be to institute a public relations program that softens the market, provide consumers with the right tool, or compel management to make the most powerful connections, find the best first investors, or hire the highest-quality staff. Whatever the method may be, the successful don't think in terms of hard work (even though they *are*, of course, willing to work hard). Instead, they figure out how to work "smart" and handle the situation by finding and using the right approach until they succeed. The unsuccessful always find work to be difficult because they never take enough time to improve their approach and make it easier on themselves. The first three years of my life as a salesperson was hard work and gave me sporadic results at best. Then I committed two years and thousands of dollars to improving my approach—and selling was no longer "work"!

Successful people invest time, energy, and money in improving themselves. As a result, they don't focus on how hard the work is but rather on how rewarding the results are! When you are winning because you have perfected your approach, it won't feel like work; it will feel like success. And nothing tastes as good as the victory of success.

19. Break Traditional Ideas

The most successful of the successful go beyond the concept of mere change and challenge traditional thinking. Look at organizations like Google, Apple, and Facebook, and you will see companies that challenge traditions and create new ways of doing things. They break that which already works in order to get to a better place. The most successful are looking to *create* traditions—not follow already established ones. Do not be a prisoner of the thinking agreed upon by others. Figure out ways to take advantage of the traditional thinking that holds others back.

The successful are called "thought leaders" who design the future with forward thinking. I built my first company on the notion of breaking traditional ideas that one industry had long accepted by showing it a better way to take care of customers. Highly successful individuals are not concerned with the way things "have always been done"; they're interested in finding new and better ways. They look at why automobiles, airplanes, newspapers, and homes have changed so little over the past 50 years and try to determine ways to create new markets. A word of warning: These people are also able to maintain their companies' existing structures while disputing conventional concepts and bringing new products to market. They don't suggest change for the sake of change; they do so in order to design superior products, relationships, and environments. The successful are willing to challenge tradition in order to discover new and better ways to accomplish their goals and dreams.

20. Be Goal-Oriented

A goal is some desirable objective—typically something yet to be achieved—that a person or company needs in order to move forward. Successful people are highly goal-oriented and always pay more attention to the target than the problem. They are seemingly able to bend bullets because of their commitment and focus on the goal. Far too many folks spend more time planning what they will get at the grocery store than they do setting the most important goals of their lives. *If you don't stay focused on your goals, you will spend your life achieving the objectives of other people—particularly those who are goal-oriented.*

Goals are incredibly important to me. I begin and finish each day by writing them down and reviewing them. Any time I encounter failure or a challenge, I take out a legal pad and write my goals down again. This helps keep my attention on where I desire to go and the goals I want to achieve—instead of letting me dwell on the difficulty of the moment. The ability to remain focused on the goal and keep your orientation on that goal's achievement is *vital* to success. Although I try to stay focused on the present, I want to keep most of my attention on the bigger picture of my goals rather than on just the task I'm accomplishing at that moment.

21. Be on a Mission

Whereas the unsuccessful spend their lives thinking in terms of a job, successful people approach their activities as though they are on a religious mission—not as work or merely "a job." Successful employees, employers, entrepreneurs, and market changers consider their daily activities to be part of a more important mission that will change things significantly. They are always thinking bigger and homing in on some massive target to achieve. Until you start approaching your job as though you are on a mission, it will always be reduced to "just a job." You must undertake every activity with the zealous attitude that this endeavor could forever change the world. Approach every phone call, e-mail, sales visit, meeting, presentation, and day you spend at the office not as a job but as a calling for which you will forever be known. Until you adopt this attitude, you will forever be stuck in a job—and probably one that isn't very fulfilling.

22. Have a High Level of Motivation

Motivation refers to the act or state of being stimulated toward action. To succeed, it is critical that you be stimulated, excited, and driven to some action or actions. Although the definition of motivation suggests that there's a reason behind the action, the study of successful people also makes it apparent that their high levels of activity are fueled by being goal-focused and mission-driven. The unsuccessful demonstrate low levels of motivation, wandering, and lack of clarity or purpose. Elevated motivation is obviously critical to 10X actions and persistence. This isn't the kind of enthusiasm that lasts for a few hours, a day, or a week; it's based on what you do *each day* to stimulate yourself toward actions and inspire yourself to keep going. Highly successful people continually seek and uncover reasons to stay perpetually provoked to new levels of success. This may be why successful people are never satisfied. As they continue to be compelled by new reasons to move forward, they achieve these new goals and then regenerate for the next round. They are constantly stimulated to higher levels of action and achievements.

There's one question I get in my seminars more than any other: "How do you stay motivated?" The answer? I create

new reasons to keep showing up. The unsuccessful unceas-
ingly suggest, "If I had what [that person] had, I would retire."
But I don't believe this claim for a second. First of all, they
don't know if that's true, since they can't tell how they'd
respond to success. It is possible—and highly probable—that
the success they'd create would also include some responsibilities and obligation to continue to produce in order to keep
things going. Motivation is an inside job. I can't motivate you,
and you can't motivate anyone else. You can encourage, you
can challenge, and you can inspire, but true motivation—the
underlying reason for doing something—must come from
within. I do it by setting goals daily to keep myself enthused.
I look at things that seem to be out of reach for me—not
just material things but other people's accomplishments and
achievements—to keep my attention on the possibilities.
Anything you can do to stay highly motivated will be critical
to your 10X commitment.

23. Be Interested in Results

Successful people don't value effort or work or time spent on
an activity; they value the results. Unsuccessful individuals
attach great importance to the time they spend at work and
their attempts at getting results—even if nothing happens.
The difference here is connected to the concept of being
unreasonable. Let's face it: Like it or not, the results are all that
matter. If you "attempt" to take out the trash but only make it
to your front hall, garbage will continue to accumulate in your
home—and you will have a problem. Until you become completely, unreasonably fixated with only getting results, you will
fall short of achieving what you desire. Quit patting yourself
on the back for trying, and save your rewards and accolades
for actual accomplishment. Drive yourself so that no one else
has to. Be hard on yourself and never let yourself off the hook
until you get results. Results (not efforts)—regardless of the

challenges, resistance, and problems—are a primary focus of the successful.

24. Have Big Goals and Dreams

Successful people dream big and have immense goals. They are not realistic. They leave that to the masses, who fight for leftovers. The second question of the 10X Rule asks: How *big* are your goals and dreams? The middle class are taught to be realistic, whereas the successful think in terms of how extensively they can spread themselves. The greatest regret of my life is that I initially set targets and goals based on what was realistic rather than on giant, radical thinking. "Big think" changes the world. It is what makes Facebook, Twitter, Google—or whatever's coming next. Realistic thinking, small goals, and trivial dreams simply won't provide you with any motivation—and they'll land you smack dab in the middle, competing with the masses. Dream big, go big, and then figure out how to go bigger than that! Read everything you can about great people and great companies' accomplishments. Surround yourself with everything you can that inspires you to think big, act big, and reach your full potential.

25. Create Your Own Reality

The successful are a lot like magicians; they don't deal in other people's realities. Instead, they are bent on creating a new reality for themselves that is different from the one that others accept. They aren't interested in what other people deem possible or impossible; they only care about producing the things they dream are possible. They're never sold on the idea of dealing in others' beliefs or guidelines, and they don't submit to the agreed-upon "reality." They want to create what they want and have a high disregard—even dislike—for mass agreement. Do a bit of research and you will see that those who have made it really big created a reality that did not exist before they came along. Whether it is a salesperson, an athlete, an artist, a politician, or an inventor, greatness is achieved by those who think nothing of being practical and are instead obsessed with the idea of creating the reality they want to make. The next reality of how things will or can be is only as far away as the next person who creates it.

26. Commit First—Figure Out Later

At first glance, this might be appear to be a highly undesirable—even perilous—trait of the highly successful. However, it's far less dangerous than the alternative frequently practiced by the unsuccessful. Most people assume that they have to figure everything out first and will commit once they do; however, they never seem to get around to it. Even when they do figure it out and are ready to commit, they usually find that the opportunity no longer exists or that someone else has claimed the spoils.

Committing first means getting 100 percent behind whatever it is you are committing to *before* you figure out every detail. This is what allows small companies and wild entrepreneurs to outmaneuver other bigger, richer competitors. The great companies of yesterday get so powerful and so enamored of layers of management that their staff spends most of its days in meetings—which causes them to become cautious and incapable of pulling triggers the way they did when they were taking risks and growing. Although it can be dicey to commit first and figure the rest out later, it is my belief that creativity and problem solving are stimulated only *after* a person fully commits. Although preparation and training are critical, challenges of the marketplace will require you to act before you determine how to make it turn out all right. It is not necessarily the smartest and brightest who win in the game of life but rather those who can commit the most passionately to their cause.

27. Be Highly Ethical

This is an area of confusion for many people—especially when they see supposedly successful individuals going to jail. Well, as far as I'm concerned, it doesn't matter how much success you amass. Going to jail would be an immediate disqualifier. Even if a criminal does not get caught, he or she is still criminal—and therefore incapable of real success. I know people who would never tell a lie or steal a penny who I don't consider ethical—because they also don't bother to fulfill their commitments as providers of security and role models for their families and friends. If you don't go to work every day—and do everything within your power to succeed—then you are stealing from your family, future, and the company for which you work. You have made agreements—either implied or spoken—with your spouse, family, colleagues, managers, and clients. The more success you create, the better you are able to take care of those agreements. To me, being ethical doesn't just mean playing by society's agreed-upon rules. I also believe that being ethical requires people to do what they have told others they *would* do—and doing so until they get the desired results. Making an effort without a result is not ethical because it is a form of lying to yourself and failing to fulfill your obligations and commitments. Trying, wishing, praying, hoping, and wanting aren't going to get you there. In my mind, ethical people achieve the results they desire and create so much success for themselves, their family, and their company that they can survive any storm and succeed regardless of any difficulty.

One of the personal experiences of which I am most proud was my ability to weather two years in a severely challenging economic environment while I was confronting other, even more serious challenges in my life—and was still able to expand my company and provide for my family. Anything short of providing long-term success means putting everyone in your life—including yourself—at risk.

I am not talking about "cash register" ethics here but rather the bigger concept of living up to your abilities and potential as well as your unspoken or explicit commitments. Merely agreeing to be a father, husband, entrepreneur, or business owner—or whatever role you play—brings with it implied commitments and agreements. I consider it unethical not to fully utilize the gifts, talents, and mind with which I have been blessed. Only you can decide what is ethical to you. However, I would suggest that any disparity between what you know you can do and what you are achieving is an ethical issue. The most successful among us are driven by ethical obligation and motivation to do something significant that aligns with their potential.

28. Be Interested in the Group

You can only do as well as the people around you. If everyone around you is sick, underperforming, and struggling, then sooner or later, you will become afflicted like everyone else. For example, pensions are strangling city and state governments because handfuls of people were interested in their own situation and didn't consider the impact it would have on the group as a whole. This type of "me first" thinking—that has no regard for the group—ultimately stifles the very group upon which an individual depends for survival. This self-serving approach later makes it almost impossible for the group to survive—and puts even that which was promised at peril.

The larger population's health and well-being should be of utmost importance to each individual member—which is something that the most successful know. You can only be as successful as the individuals with whom you involve and associate yourself. It doesn't matter what position you hold— whether you are leading a group or are part of a group—your success is limited to the ability of those around you. This does not mean that successful people aren't interested in themselves. It's just that they realize that they have to expend energy and express interest in their associates because they know that if they are not doing well, even the most well-to-do will be dragged down with them. It is actually self-serving, to some degree, to care about what happens to everyone else. You want everyone on your team winning and improving because this is likely to improve your game. For that reason, you always want to do everything you can to bring the rest of the team to higher levels.

29. Be Dedicated to Continuous Learning

The most successful CEOs are reported to read an average of 60 books and attend more than six conferences per year—whereas the average American worker reads an average of less than one book and makes 319 times less income. Although the media often discuss the disparity between the rich and the poor, they frequently fail to cover the amount of time and energy the wealthy have committed to reading, studying, and educating themselves. Successful people make time for conventions, symposiums, and reading. There has never been a book, audio program, download, webinar, or speech from which I have not benefited—even from the ones that sucked.

The most successful people I know read everything they can get their hands on. They approach a $30 book as though it has the potential to make them a million dollars. They see every opportunity to train and educate themselves as the most solid and sure investment they can make. Unsuccessful people, on the other hand, simply worry about the cost of a book or seminar without ever giving consideration to the benefits it will provide. So join the ranks of successful people who know that their income, wealth, health, and future are dependent upon their ability to continue to seek out new information and never stop learning.

30. Be Uncomfortable

Those who succeed were—at one point or another in their lives—willing to put themselves in situations that were uncomfortable, whereas the unsuccessful seek comfort from all their decisions. The most important things I have done in my life were *not* the things I was comfortable doing; in fact, many of them made me very uneasy. Whether it was moving to a new city, cold calling a client, meeting new people, doing a new presentation, or venturing into new sectors, most of it was uncomfortable for me until I got used to doing it. It is so tempting to become content with your surroundings, daily rituals, and habits—most of which are probably not furthering your mission. It feels good when things are familiar. However, successful people are willing to put themselves in new and unfamiliar situations. That doesn't mean that they are always changing just for the sake of changing; however, they know that getting too comfortable, too relaxed, and too familiar causes a person to become soft and lose his or her creativity and hunger to stay out front. So be willing to be uncomfortable, and do what makes other people uncomfortable as well. It is a sure sign that you're on your way to success.

31. "Reach Up" in Relationships

If it were up to me, this would be a basic course for every year that someone attended school. It would include drills in which people are encouraged to do things that they are not comfortable doing. The successful constantly talk about having people around them who are smarter, brighter, and more creative. It's unlikely that you'll hear one of them say, "I got here by surrounding myself with more people just like me." Yet the average person typically spends his or her time with like-minded people or even those who bring less to the table than they can.

Make a habit of "reaching up" in all of your relationships—toward people who are better connected, better educated, and even more successful. These individuals have much more to share than your supposed "equals." This habit is connected to their willingness to change, challenge tradition, grow, and do what others can't fathom. Reach up—never sideways and *never* down! You must base your decisions on what will be the greatest investment to move you toward your ethical commitment to create success for yourself, your family, and your business. The people with whom you surround yourself will have a great deal to do with whether you achieve your goals—or not. You don't want to go horizontal. You want to go up—and you do this by associating yourself with bigger thinkers, bigger dreamers, and bigger players. Black belts don't learn new skills from white belts. They can be reminded of the basics, but a white belt cannot take the black belt to a red belt. And you can't become a scratch golfer by playing with bogie golfers. You have to interact with people who are better than you. It's the only way to become better yourself.

32. Be Disciplined

Remember: We are not just talking about money here. This refers to being successful in all areas of life—and to do so, you will not be able to compromise this thing called discipline. Discipline is an orderly, prescribed conduct that will get you what you want—and it's a requirement for 10X players. Unfortunately, most peoples' disciplines look more like bad habits instead of the—admittedly uncomfortable—10X actions they should be taking over and over again.

Discipline is what you use to complete any activity until the activity—regardless of how uncomfortable—becomes your normal operating procedure. In order to ever attain and keep success, you must determine which habits are constructive—and discipline both yourself and your group (see point 28) to do those things over and over again.

If you find you do not have all of the previously mentioned success traits and habits—or you see yourself having most or some of them most of the time but occasionally fall off a bit—no worries. I would expect that most of the people reading this don't consistently display every single one of these qualities *all* the time. Become aware of what the list is, keep it close to you, and make a new commitment to making these techniques part of *who you are* rather than merely something you "do." Although I don't personally operate in the success column 100 percent of the time, I do make efforts to ensure that I spend most of my time doing what successful people do.

None of the things on this list is a superhuman quality. Every single one is attainable. Don't use just one or two of the techniques. Start thinking and operating with them, and they will become a part of you. Use them all.

Exercise

Without looking, name five traits of successful people and their counterparts.

_____

_____

_____

What do you do best now?

_____

_____

_____

What do you need to work on more?

_____

_____

_____

23

Getting Started with 10X

So where do you even get started with all this? What kinds of challenges might you run into? And how do you make 10X a truly persistent discipline? All you really have to do is look at the list of what successful people do to determine what you need to do. When to start? Well, remember: There are only two times that exist for successful people. You want to focus to some degree on now but keep most of your attention on the future you desire to create. You certainly can't start yesterday, and if you wait until tomorrow, you won't be a success because you will have violated an important tenet of the successful: Act now and then keep acting with the knowledge that enough actions taken now will create the future. When successful people become lazy, they add time to their decisions. At that point, they are probably more concerned with protecting what they have than with creating new levels of success. And conservation of success or what to do with it once you get it is not what this book is about!

I wrote this book at 52 years of age and have currently created enough success for myself, only to have an appetite for more. I truly believe that I have yet to entirely fulfill my capacity or abilities. I don't want it just for the game or the money but mostly because I really do consider it to be an ethical obligation to utilize my potential. Whatever—or whoever—drives you, go get it now—and quit being reasonable with yourself.

I am undertaking a major personal and professional expansion as I write this—all while expanding my family and my philanthropic desires. Everyone in my organization and even my clients will tell you that when I go at something, I always go *now* with an unreasonable belief to do *whatever* is necessary to hit my targets. I am not an organizer, a great planner, or a manager. I realize that taking action without adding time, meetings, and overanalysis is both an asset and a deficiency. The people who know me would probably also tell you that when I embark on a project—whether it is writing a new book, creating a seminar program, developing a new product, starting a new workout, improving my marriage, or spending time with my daughter—I go at it *completely*. I'm all in, fully committed, like a hungry dog on the back of a meat truck. I know myself fairly well. When I get involved in something, I am completely unreasonable with the actions I take until I get the results I want. I don't make excuses for myself, nor do I let others make excuses.

Now means *now*—not a minute from now. Start with first things first; make your initial list of goals, then a list of actions that will propel you in that direction. Then—*without* overthinking it—start taking those actions. A few things to keep in mind as you start:

1. Do not reduce your goals as you write them.
2. Do not get lost in the details of how to accomplish them at this point.
3. Ask yourself, "What actions can I take today to move me toward these goals?"

4. Take whatever actions you come up with—regardless of what they are or how you feel.

5. Do not prematurely value the outcome of your actions.

6. Go back each day and review the list.

As you get started on this path of 10X, you may feel a bit overwhelmed. You might even notice a tendency to start talking yourself out of getting started and taking action. Don't be tempted to wait. You know it doesn't work to delay. Think of yourself like being a car stuck in the mud; you need just enough traction to move an inch, and then you can begin to get out. It may require that you get dirty—but it's certainly better than being stuck.

As I've mentioned previously, you want to be aware of friends and family who offer supposed "advice" because they love and care about you. Many of them may suggest that they don't want you to be "unrealistic" and then disappointed. The vocabulary and mind-set of average people, even those you love, is always the same—be careful, play it safe, don't be impractical, success isn't everything, be satisfied with what you have, life is to be lived, money won't make you happy, don't want so much, take it easy, you don't have experience, you're too young, you're too old—and on and on. When you hear what average people say and think, thank them for their advice. Then remind them that you want their support in going for it, and let them know that you would rather commit to your dreams and goals and be disappointed than never commit and be disappointed.

Let me give you a real-life example of using 10X that took place for me as I was writing this book. You'll see as you read the following scenario how I was able to employ many of the habits and traits of the successful to reach the goals I had set for myself—and even go beyond what I had initially imagined. Sometime before I wrote my last book, *If You're Not First, You're Last*, I realized that although I had habitually been taking massive action in my life, I had yet to really think in 10X magnitudes. So I decided to test out my 10X Rule as I wrote this book. As I reset my targets to match 10X thinking, I realized that one of my goals was to become *the* name that is synonymous with sales training. I wanted to become the person who people think of *first* when they consider sales training, sales motivation, strategies—anything to do with selling. This was the concept of domination that I had in mind as I wrote *If You're Not First, You're Last.* I had my new, considerable goal in place—but no clue as to how to accomplish it. I know, however, that had I stopped and tried to figure out "how" to do this before I committed to making it my goal, I never would have gotten started. I probably would have decided immediately that it was impossible.

Once I clarified the right-sized target and avoided overwhelming myself with technicalities and "how" minutiae, I then allowed the target to determine which actions would be most consistent with its size. It seemed as though a big enough goal would automatically move me to the right actions. A little trick I used was to ask myself quality questions like "What do I have to do to become *the name* people think of when it comes to the topic of sales?" I immediately began writing down answers and ideas: (a) Get 6 billion people to know who I am. (b) Get a TV show. (c) Get a radio show. (d) Get my books into every book store and library. (e) Get on all the major talk shows and news shows. (f) Make *If You're Not First, You're Last* a *New York Times* best-seller. (g) Make a major push using social media to have people around the world become acquainted with my name. Again, I didn't know how to do any of this at this point—nor did I want to figure it out during these early steps. I know I would only become derailed by the "how tos" and the "cannots," and I just wanted to focus on hitting my target.

As I considered my goal of becoming synonymous with selling, I knew I was setting a target big enough to keep me interested. I was inspired to do anything consistent with the answers we developed to our quality questions. Every single action my company and I took was aimed at getting my name out there. We didn't know anything or have any connections to television. I had written two self-published books but didn't even know how to get a book published, much less sold in book stores. At this time, I hadn't done any TV/news or media interviews and assumed that sites like Facebook and Twitter were for people who didn't have anything better to do. Yet of all the goals I had listed, I firmly believed that getting a TV show would have the biggest bang. I know that all the actions I took were somehow connected and were going to be vital.

I immediately went to my wife and informed her that I was somehow going to get a TV show where I could demonstrate my ability to enter any company anywhere and sell anything in any economy—and increase that company's sales. I knew that this would help me avoid any potential obscurity among sales organizations worldwide. Without reservation, she responded, "That would make an incredible TV show! You'd be great—let's do it! How can I help?" No questions asked—just full support.

I was extremely excited, but I did everything I could not to share my new idea with anyone who might tell me it was impossible. I realized this was a big and exciting enough challenge to get all my resources behind. I also knew it wouldn't take place overnight.

My first move was to inform my team—and emphasize that any project that moved us in the direction of our target had to get done. I made it clear that I didn't want to hear "I can't, we can't, it's too hard, it can't be done." We started making 10X moves by making calls to anyone we knew who could put me in touch with someone involved in the media, television, and book industries. This was somewhat of a painful step. People who work in the book and television industries have seen more than their share of failures and have therefore come to view projects like this in a fairly pessimistic light. They didn't hesitate to let me know—multiple times—how long something like this would take and that I couldn't set my expectations too high. I was hammered by the average kind of thinking ingrained in so many people—the very kind that keeps them from accomplishing what they want. I repeatedly received comments like "300 shows are pitched for every single show that gets picked up," "The networks aren't spending money," "A sales show is not a topic people care about," "There are over 750,000 books written a year," "When you don't have a well-known name, getting on TV is very difficult," and on and on.

Although this might be about the time when many people consider giving up, I didn't—and you can't either. Realize that everyone who's trying to get their "break" is going through the same thing. I had to continually disregard the naysayers and refocus on my goals. I would look again at what I had to do to accomplish that goal and then do it—regardless of whether I was scared or comfortable. Remember: Successful people embrace fear and discomfort!

I don't know if it was because of what we were doing or because we kept our focus on what we wanted, but I think it had to be a combination of both. I hired my first PR firm, and even though it was a complete disappointment, I didn't give up, because I knew it was important. When the second one didn't work out, I hired another one. We were undertaking a lot of projects simultaneously; they all took time, energy, money, and creativity, and they were all new to us. I had no way to gauge whether it was going to work or not. Additionally, I was doing this at a time when the economy was terrible. Everyone was contracting. My company—and the economy at large—was experiencing the greatest economic reduction I'd seen in my lifetime. My clients were reducing employees by up to 40 percent. My best competitor cut his staff in half, and countless others literally shut their doors. Entire companies were collapsing—and even complete industries were at risk. Everyone was scared, but I kept one important point in mind: that the most successful expand while others get smaller. They take risks while others conserve. So rather than cut my staff or cut our expansion, I eliminated my own salary—and took the money I normally paid myself and used it to fund 10X.

Even as I was challenged like never before on every front imaginable, I did everything I could just to keep the target in focus. It wasn't easy, and there was no guaranteed outcome, but I did everything I could to remind myself that we could make it happen. The more committed I became, the more challenges I faced. I almost felt as though the universe was just trying to see how strong I was and whether I could stick to it. My PR firms would get me one measly interview in three months, the banks were asking for more and more money, and my income had been cut off (by me, of course—but it still hurt!). The only thing I had going for me was my marriage, a new baby coming into the world, and my fierce belief in my capacity to persist and work. I was in love with my 10X goal. I knew it wasn't just good for me but that the world needed to know a new way of doing things. To me, it wasn't just an issue of personal success; it was about being on a mission to help. The entire world was suffering economically. I felt that my goal was substantial enough to move the bar in a big way—and not just for me. I felt that the risk of expansion was worth more than the money or the energy I was expending. *The goal has to be more valuable than the risk—or you have determined the wrong target.*

So I continued with my commitment, dealt with the fear, became a fanatic about it, and continued to increase actions in other areas. I didn't control the PR, the television networks, or the publishing companies, so I went to work on what I *could* control. Everywhere I could get my message out, I did—and finally we started seeing results.

We started getting calls to do radio shows and even some TV interviews. One morning, I got a phone call from CNN Radio to do an interview on the topic of the Fannie Mae bust, and I of course agreed. The next morning, I was asked to show up at 3:30 AM at the studio for an interview on the foreclosure problem, and I said, "*Yes*, no problem—I am your boy!" I remember getting a call from the PR people asking, "Can you talk about the LeBron James contract and how it will affect basketball?" I said yes and headed off to the NBC studios without delay. Ten minutes before I arrived, I received a phone call in which I was informed, "The topic has been changed. Instead of LeBron, you will be talking about the relationship between Levi Johnston and Sarah Palin." I didn't know anything about Levi Johnston, but I still did the interview. The topic didn't matter to me; I just wanted these media sources to know that they could count on me to show up and deliver. I reminded myself that the goal was not to do an interview on CNBC or to talk about Levi but to get the world's attention—so that people would start to think of me the moment they thought about selling. Although none of this coverage would make me money, it would—more importantly—make me known.

We then started pushing on the social media front in a huge way. We pushed so hard that I had customers, friends, and even employees complaining that I was sending out too many e-mails and creating too many posts. Rather than backing off, I increased the amount of e-mails and posts until the complaints turned into admiration. I went from being disappointed with PR to being overbooked (that was just one way my massive action created new problems).

I kept making efforts toward the TV show as well. I tried to meet with theatrical agents, managers, big agencies, and little agencies, but even they wouldn't meet with me. I talked to friends in Hollywood who had experience with the TV channels—and who had been unsuccessfully pitching their own reality TV shows for years. Yet even as I was venturing into this new space, I continued to add wood to the things I could control: speaking engagements, client calls, e-mails, social media, article writing, and my regular core business activities. And every time I would get disappointed or experienced a setback, I would go back and write down my goals. This forced me to remain focused on the destination instead of the difficulties. I always kept in mind that the successful keep their eye on their targets regardless of the challenges.

Then, one day I got a phone call from a casting agent with a group in New York who informed me, "We ran across one of your videos on YouTube and think you would be perfect for a TV show. We've been looking for someone like you but haven't been able to find the right person." My response? "I *am* the right person! What took you so long to find me?" I then got the name of the person in charge of the project, called him, and told him that it just so happened that I was going to be in New York that weekend—immediately establishing a commitment to the project. (By the way, I did not have a trip to New York planned prior to this call. However, I did have it in my mind to meet with someone about a TV show. Funny how things work out, huh?) The producer told me that he would love to meet with me. I told him I would be there at the end of the week and got off the phone.

I immediately showed the producer my willingness and hunger to make things go right and was willing to commit without having "all the information." Remember: Successful people commit first and figure the rest out later. Some people might claim that it was entirely too impetuous of me to jump on the chance and claim that I'd be in New York within a week. But my calendar is mine to schedule whatever I want, whenever I want. And because I am committed completely to my success as my duty, I decided that "New York trip" was going on my calendar. I don't need a personal assistant or a computer to do that for me. Give yourself every advantage, and give the person on the other end every opportunity to move forward. Don't add time, hesitation, and doubt. Get everyone in your life reading from the same playbook. Don't wait until something good happens and then have to add time by checking with others or your calendar. This will only slow your momentum down. Be constantly prepared for success so that you can grab the opportunity when it comes along!

Once I got off the phone with the producer, I called my assistant and told her to get me to New York. She informed me that I already had another commitment that I was unable to reschedule. *New problems—Yeah!* So I immediately picked up the phone (the "do-it-now" strategy) and used this problem to have more contact with my new opportunity (customer acquisition vs. customer satisfaction). I made the call and told New York that I couldn't make it out there as soon as I thought and proposed another time. Interestingly, the new time actually turned out to be better for them as well. I flew to NY on my dime (take risk) and had no clue what I was doing (so what). When I got there, I found out the company owner was tied up in another meeting. I persuaded my contact to ask the owner to make just 10 minutes of face time for me (unreasonable). I pleaded with his gatekeepers, "Guys, I spent longer in the security line at the airport than I am asking him for—I need 10 minutes to explain my vision for the show." The owner reluctantly made the time—and within five minutes, I could tell he was completely thrilled about the concept. He then spent an hour with me, and I was certain he would go to bat for me. On my way out the door, he said to me, "Anyone with this much belief and clarity I will get behind." The group then decided to start pitching the concept to networks.

Not long after that, I received another phone call from a group here in LA connected with reality TV producer Mark Burnett. They asked me to be a guest on the Joan Rivers show, *How Did You Get So Rich?* (which was somewhat ridiculous to me, because I don't consider myself that rich). But, of course, I agreed to the show. Just before the Joan Rivers people came out to shoot the episode, the group in New York sent out a crew to interview me for material to use with the networks. When it was over, I called my new best buddies in New York and gave them my feedback: "The interview went well—but there is no way this will sell the show. The studio heads need to meet with me so that I can sell it myself, or we need to shoot me actually *going into* a company and increasing their sales for real and capturing it on camera." I received a response that they "normally don't shoot this" until they get some level of interest from a network. However, I went on to explain that the interview was too soft, and I really needed to create a short video that would show the networks that this wouldn't be a show about me. It would be a show that everyone would want to watch, demonstrating exactly how to create success in any business in any city and during the worst economy in 100 years.

To keep fueling the fire, I would continue to send both groups new information. I happened to be in Las Vegas at a convention (taking care of my core business) and noticed a camera crew shooting. I told the crew about what I was trying to do with this TV show and that I wanted to send my associates in New York a three-minute piece. I asked them to record an impromptu video of me that would get their attention. I told them that if it worked, they would know they helped me make a TV show a reality. Surprisingly, they agreed.

I then recorded a three-minute video that I labeled "You Can't Handle the Truth" that you can find on YouTube. The crew was kind enough to cut me a copy to send to both groups, and they loved it. This kept them thinking about me and furthering my cause. This video even caused the group in New York to broaden those networks they were planning to pitch to.

My commitment to move the ball forward was starting to stoke their commitment and enthusiasm as well. I was adding wood to my fire—and certainly going beyond the socially agreed-upon norms. Just so you know, I also—for the most part—had no idea what I was doing (courage is created through actions). The only thing I knew was that I was taking action that would accomplish the bigger goal. I was scared, worried about money I was investing, and feared rejection along the way but knew that I was creating an entirely new set of problems—which, of course, was a signal that I was making some of the right moves.

The next major event occurred when Joan Rivers came out to my house to shoot her episode with me. I, of course, shared with her my idea about a show, and she gave me the names of the guys who produced her show. I employed the method of reaching up, not sideways and down. I called the group in LA and requested a meeting to pitch this idea—just in case the guys in New York couldn't see the project through. Remember: Never quit adding wood and taking action, regardless of what others are doing.

The group in LA liked the idea. It also didn't hurt that the producers had already seen what I did on the Joan Rivers show. By this point, I had gone from a single idea with minimal support to having not one but *two* companies considering the possibility of a show. I was in complete self-doubt when I went to Paramount and kept thinking, "These guys are just seeing me because they feel a bit obligated. So don't think for a moment that you can be confident and secure every step of the way." I literally almost cancelled my trip to Paramount on the way over, thinking it was just a waste—when my sense of duty kicked in. Yes, I was scared and didn't really know what I was doing, but I did it anyway. I had to remember that emotions are overrated, and the boogeyman's job is to keep me down. Again, pay attention to all the successful strategies I am illustrating here because they are what guided my decisions and should guide yours.

Upon meeting members of the group, I was shocked to find they had already spent time coming up with their own version of a show with me. All my fears about their lack of interest—like most fears—were completely unfounded. When both of these groups researched me, they both commented, "It is like you are everywhere" (omnipresence).

Although I clearly wanted to shout from the rooftops at this point, I knew I couldn't get too excited or stop to celebrate. I had to keep pushing with more actions and more responsibility in order to move things forward. Rather than waiting for one of the two companies to offer me a deal, I started calling retail companies to see if I could line up organizations that would be interested in being on my new show (that, by the way, I don't have yet). Although this would normally be the production company's job, (1) there was no deal or company to do this yet, (2) I hate waiting, and (3) I wanted to move things forward to a point where no one could walk away. Was I being too aggressive, acting in a socially unacceptable way, and breaking the agreed-upon rules? Could this offend someone? Absolutely! Look, if either of these groups said no to me, none of what I was doing would matter to them anyway!

It was interesting that when we called companies to let them know about the show, not only were people interested in being on it, they also started asking us how we could help them before the show. We landed multiple new accounts just by making the calls about the show. I then informed the New York group that I was lining up organizations that wanted to be involved in the show. The producers told me to "slow down," to which I replied, "I can tell you I will—but I won't." What did come out of this call was that the group in NY agreed to shoot a teaser piece of the show. We all agreed that a Harley dealership would make for a great visual and fantastic story. After a dozen phone calls, we found a company willing to agree—but I still didn't have a commitment from New York. Yet once I told them that I had the ideal place ready to go, they couldn't say no. They agreed to send a crew to shoot me for two days. (Understand that when you keep pushing forward, something will result.)

I found myself with no experience shooting a TV show, no script, no notes, no preparation, and really no idea of what we were actually going to do, but I was on my way to shoot two days in the largest Harley store in the world (commit first; figure the rest out later). I was working with a group of people I had never worked with, and frankly, I was scared to death. The only thing I knew for sure was that I could go into any company and increase its sales. I kept one thing in mind: Fear is an indicator that you are moving in the right direction.

To put myself at ease, I focused my attention on the future and reminded myself of my goals. On the way over, I reminded myself repeatedly that I could handle my fears and that I was going to have to do something like this. Otherwise, people would never come to know about me and my ability to help people. Remember: Your only real problem is obscurity. I kept giving myself pep talks: "Show up, be all in, and trust that creativity follows commitment." Look at the number of successful traits that I employed here: have a "can do" attitude; believe that it will be successful; show up; commit first, figure the rest out later; do it now, not later; go in all the way; be courageous; do what you fear; stay focused on the target; and be willing to be uncomfortable. Even if I failed, I knew that my mind-set and actions were in the right place. I may regret my performance—but at least I won't regret not taking a shot!

We started shooting the "teaser." About three hours into it, the producer said, "Grant we need something that really shows what you do, beyond words, beyond explanations. We need to see that what you teach actually happens." I looked at the camera man and said, "Turn on that camera and follow me." I then took over the Harley showroom floor by going from customer to customer and engaging each of them. I had clients getting on and off the bikes. I was moving them around, taking photos of them, and texting photos to their spouses at home with messages like "I am about to sell your husband a motorcycle." It was fun, easy, and incredibly powerful to interact with customers and handle their objections, resistance, and problems—and then have it all recorded on camera.

At the end of the first day, the producer looked at me and asked, "Can you do this with any company, anywhere?" I'm sure you know by now what I told him, but just in case you don't, I'll repeat it here: "Dude, I can do this in any company, anywhere, endless times and show anyone, selling anything, how to increase their sales in any economy!" He said, "I believe you—and I believed in you before I even saw what you just did. Now America has to see this TV show."

I asked him for one favor: "Once you get an agreement to meet with the network people, allow me to pitch it to them." I knew that I could sell this show better than anyone else. He agreed, went back to New York, and started editing the piece. He called me the following week and told me how excited he was but that the summer season was going to delay his presentations to networks. He explained that it would probably be another four weeks before he could pitch the reel, but he assured me that everyone will love it.

I hadn't heard from him for about three weeks, so I started calling him. I knew I wouldn't get anywhere with this project without persistence. When we spoke, he confirmed that he was still "all in." I reminded him of his commitment to me to let me pitch it to the executives. He called me back a week later, at 6:45 AM, and told me the following: "Grant I have bad news. The networks don't want you to come pitch the show. Instead, they want to start shooting right away."

The first thing I thought of was the guy who had told me, "For every TV show that gets made, 300 are pitched." The second thing I thought of was the person who told me that no one wanted to see a show on sales. (Stay focused on the future, be unreasonable about it, continue to add wood, and don't focus on what people say has been done, can be done, or is possible!) People are so caught up in their own negativity and losses that they give up on creating the future they want. Others feel the need to criticize other peoples' ventures as a way to justify giving up on their own. Never regard the impossible; instead, stay focused on what you can do to make the supposedly impossible possible. It is a good thing I didn't bother to listen to all the naysayers, huh?

At this point in time, we haven't yet shot the show, but everything is in place to do so, and we expect a release in the upcoming year. My hope is that this show will provide viewers with the direction that regular people need in order to create success in any economy, anywhere, and at anytime. Market slowdowns, financial problems, challenges, and fear are not as powerful as a person's ability to dream big and act at 10X levels! No economy, no matter how bad, can hold down a goal that is followed by enough action.

I've shared this story with you to show you how I employed many of the concepts discussed in this book in order to achieve the goal of expanding my footprint. I am just like you—no more talented and no more certain—but I am using 10X thinking and taking 10X actions. This isn't just a book; this is what you have to do today in order to make it. The world no longer rewards talk. You and I must not just talk the talk but walk the walk. This should help you realize that 10X *will work* for anyone.

This short story isn't even really about me; it is a guide for what *you* have to do. You have no idea how many people throughout my life have laughed, criticized, and raised their eyebrows about the things I wanted to do. You don't know about the hundreds of thousands of phone calls I have made that went nowhere or the thousands of e-mails to which no one responded. You have no idea how many people—even my supporters—suggested to me that I may be pushing beyond the limits and putting myself at risk. I have spent 30 years preparing and studying, making mistakes, and taking action—all of which has allowed me to develop some level of discipline that I have not always had.

Training and learning are absolutely critical to your follow-through and the development of courage, persistence, unreasonable thinking, and especially discipline. I keep reminding myself that when it comes to dreams and goals, there is no being reasonable or rational and there is no distinguishing between the possible and the impossible. I think you will agree that it is impossible for you to ever do anything exceptional if you continue to live your life with thinking and actions that are mediocre.

Big thinking, massive actions, expansion, and risk taking are necessary for your survival and future growth. Staying small and quiet are just ways to continue being small and quiet. Keep thinking this way, and sometime in the very near future, no one will be able to see you, hear you—or be aware that you ever existed. Commit to 10X thinking and 10X action.

This is the major difference between success and the alternative. It is not about intelligence, economics, or even who you know—because without massive action, none of those things matter.

I still have many of my own long-term goals and targets to meet. I haven't yet made the show, 6 billion people do not yet know me, and there are countless other things I still want to do—many I haven't even thought of yet! However, I do know that I am moving in the right direction. I also know, and want you to know again, that this is not about me being more special or having some unique quality; it is simply about operating with 10X thinking and 10X actions.

Make your fire so big and so hot that others will have no choice but to sit around it in amazement. You will never have all the answers, your timing will never be perfect, and there will always be obstacles and difficulties. However, you can always count on one thing: Taking massive actions consistently and persistently and then following up with more fourth-degree actions are the only ways to guarantee the success you desire. Always go all in on massive action. Let the rest of the world operate at the first three degrees of action, and watch them spend their lives fighting over the bits and pieces left behind.

Look around you and you will see the world filled with average people, average thinking, and—at best—average actions. Take another look. What you will *really* see behind this acceptance of average are people who have given up on their dreams and who cease to live with a dynamic purpose. They are instead willing to settle for whatever their estimation of "normal" is. When you're choosing the people whom you will learn from, look for the exceptional—those who stand out because of the way they approach their lives. Don't worry about how they are special or different from you. Focus on how they think and act and how you can duplicate that. Success is not a choice or an option; it's your duty to operate at the right level of thoughts and actions. So follow through on your responsibility to leave a footprint on this planet—so that when you are done with your tour of duty, you will be remembered for approaching your life with nothing less than the biggest of dreams and the most remarkable actions. Remember: Success is your duty, obligation, and responsibility, and by thinking at 10X levels and taking 10X actions, I am certain you will create more success than you have even dreamed of!

Glossary

Most words have multiple meanings, so for a full understanding of each word included here, seek out a good dictionary. I have found that my ability to fully understand any subject is limited only by my understanding of the words contained in that subject. So the first thing to do, the secret to applying the 10X Rule, is to *always* understand the words and phrases of the subject you are learning. This has been a key point of my own success. When I have failed to do this, I have failed in reaching my goals.

10X Rule. Concept based on understanding the correct estimation of how much effort and thought are required to get anything done successfully. Where others perform one action, the 10X Rule says to do 10 actions and to set targets 10 times higher than you first imagine.

401(k). A retirement account to which both employee and employer contribute, on which taxes are deferred until withdrawal, and for which the employee usually selects the types of investments.

absolute. Positive; unquestionable.

abundance. An ample quantity; wealth.

accommodate. To bring into agreement or to bend to another's needs.

accomplish. (1) To bring about (a result) by effort; (2) to bring to completion; (3) to succeed.

act. The doing of a thing; deed.

action. (1) A thing done; deed; (2) the accomplishment of a thing usually over a period of time.

adapt. To make fit (as for a specific or new use or situation), often by modification.

additional. The result of adding; increase.

advertising. The action of calling something to the attention of the public, especially by paid announcements.

agreed. To concur in (as an opinion); admit, concede.

agreement. (1) A contract duly executed and legally binding; (2) spoken or unspoken mutual reality on a given situation.

air. The general character or complexion of anything; appearance.

á la carte. A menu or list wherein each item is priced separately.

alterations. The result of modification.

Amway. A direct-selling company that uses multilevel marketing or network marketing to promote its products. Amway was founded in 1959 by Jay Van Andel and Richard DeVos.

Ancient Rome. A small, agricultural community that grew into one of the largest civilizations in the ancient world. Internal strife and external attacks eventually broke it up into independent kingdoms. The Dark Ages followed this division and dispersion.

ancillary. Extra; not the main source.

annual. Covering the period of a year.

apathetic. (1) Having or showing little or no feeling or emotion; spiritless; (2) having little or no interest or concern.

arrogance. An attitude of superiority manifested in an overbearing manner or in presumptuous claims or assumptions.

assertive. Characterized by confidence.

asset. An item of value owned; (plural) the items on a balance sheet showing the book value of property owned.

assignments. Specified tasks or an amount of work assigned or undertaken as if assigned by authority.

attention. (1) Observation, notice, especially a consideration with a view to action; (2) an act of civility or courtesy, especially in courtship; (3) consideration of the needs and wants of others.

audition. A trial performance to appraise an entertainer's merits.

Barack Obama. Born August 4, 1961, Obama is the 44th and current president of the United States. He is the first African American to hold the office. Obama was the junior U.S. senator from Illinois from January 2005 until November 2008, when he resigned following his election to the presidency.

barrage. A rapid outpouring of many things at once.

basic. Constituting or serving as the basis or starting point.

basics. Something that is fundamental (e.g., get back to *basics*).

bend over backward. To go beyond the normal expectations in order to create a positive effect.

beyond. (1) On or to the farther side, farther; (2) in addition.

Bible. Books forming the central religious text of Judaism and Christianity.

Bill Gates. Born October 28, 1955, Gates is an American business magnate, philanthropist, author, and chairman of Microsoft, the software company he founded with Paul Allen. He is ranked consistently as one of the world's wealthiest people and the wealthiest overall as of March 2009. During his career at Microsoft, Gates held the positions of CEO and chief software architect, and he remains the largest individual shareholder with more than 8 percent of the common stock.

biochemical. Characterized by, produced by, or involving chemical reactions in living organisms.

biological. Study of living organisms and vital processes.

BlackBerry. A wireless handheld device introduced in 1999 as a two-way pager. In 2002, known more commonly as the smartphone.

blind. Made or done without sight of certain objects.

blip. Something relatively small or inconsequential within a larger context.

block and tackle. The simple things necessary in order to accomplish a task (comes from football terminology).

boogeyman. A folkloric or legendary ghostlike monster. The boogeyman has no specific appearance, and conceptions of the monster can vary drastically, even from household to household within the same community. In many cases, he simply *has* no set appearance in the mind of a child but is just an amorphous embodiment of terror.

briefing. An act or instance of giving precise instructions or essential information.

broke. To ruin financially; out of money.

budget. A list of all planned expenses and revenues; a plan for saving and spending.

business downturn. A downward turn, especially toward a decline in business and economic activity.

buy-in. The commitment of interested or affected parties to a decision (often called stakeholders) to "buy in" to the decision; that is, to agree to give it support, often by having been involved in its formulation.

campaign. A connected series of operations designed to bring about a particular result.

capital. (1) A stock of accumulated goods, especially at a specified time and in contrast to income received during a specified period; also the value of these accumulated goods; (2) accumulated goods devoted to the production of other goods; (3) accumulated possessions calculated to bring in income.

chaos. A state of utter confusion.

cheerleader. One who calls for and directs organized cheering.

church activities. A form of organized, supervised, often extracurricular recreation in a place of religious worship.

Circuit City. Publicly held company that sold electronics. Failed in 2009.

circumstance. The sum of essential and environmental factors (as of an event or situation).

cold call. A call made without introduction or advance notice, referred to as "cold" because no introduction has been made.

Communist Russia. The largest ruling Communist Party in the world, which collapsed in 1991.

community. A body of persons of common and especially professional interests scattered throughout a larger society.

competition. Those who strive against others to win.

competitive. The state of striving consciously or unconsciously for an objective.

conditioned. (1) Brought or put into a specified state; (2) determined or established by conditioning.

conquer. To gain mastery over or win by overcoming obstacles or opposition.

contact. A person serving as a go-between, messenger, connection, or source of special information.

contraction. The act of getting smaller; reducing efforts, resources, and energy used.

control. (1) To exercise restraining or directing influence over, regulate; (2) to have power over.

counterintuitive. Contrary to what one would intuitively expect; the power or faculty of attaining direct knowledge or cognition without evident rational thought and inference.

courage. An act that demonstrates mental or moral strength to venture, persevere, and withstand danger, fear, or difficulty.

craft. An occupation or trade requiring manual dexterity or artistic skill.

crawfish. Any of numerous freshwater crustaceans resembling the lobster but usually much smaller.

creative. Having the quality of something created rather than imitated.

critical. Of, relating to, or being a turning point or especially important juncture.

CRM (Customer Relations Manager). Software applications that allow companies to manage every aspect of their relationship with a customer.

crossover. An instance of breaking into another category.

cultivate. To encourage and help the growth of.

culture. (1) The set of shared attitudes, values, goals, and practices that characterizes an institution or organization (a corporate *culture* focused on the bottom line); (2) the set of values, conventions, or social practices associated with a particular field, activity, or societal characteristic.

customer satisfaction. Business term; a measure of how products and services supplied by a company meet or surpass customer expectations. It is seen as a key performance indicator within business and is part of the four perspectives of a balanced scorecard.

cycle (sales cycle). An interval of time during which a recurring succession of events or phenomena are completed.

database. Usually a large collection of data organized especially for rapid search and retrieval.

database management. The act of conducting or supervising usually a large collection of data.

data-scrubbing programs. The process of taking a data set with individually identifiable information and removing or altering the data in such a way that the usefulness of the data set is retained but the identification of individuals contained in that data set is nearly impossible.

dazzling. To arouse admiration by an impressive display.

deaf ears. Unwilling to hear or listen; not to be persuaded.

deal. An arrangement for mutual advantage.

defy. To confront with assured power of resistance; disregard.

degree. The relative intensity of something.

delusion. Act of misleading the mind or judgment of something. (I used this in the context of misleading yourself from falsehoods. In this way, delusion is good.)

demise. (1) A cessation of existence or activity; (2) a loss of position or status.

demographics. (1) The statistical characteristics of human populations (such as age or income) used especially to identify markets; (2) a market or segment of the population identified by demographics.

denial. A psychological defense mechanism whereby confrontation with a personal problem or reality is avoided by denying the existence of the problem or reality.

dependency. (1) The quality or state of being dependent; (2) one who is relied upon; (3) addiction.

deploy. To spread out, utilize, or arrange for a deliberate purpose.

deprived. Marked by the withholding, especially of the necessities of life or healthful environmental influences.

determine. To fix conclusively (e.g., *determine* motives).

detox. (1) To remove a harmful substance (such as a poison or toxin) or the effect of such; (2) to render (a harmful substance) harmless.

differentiate. To mark or show a difference in; constitute a difference that distinguishes.

diligence. The act characterized by steady, earnest, and energetic effort; painstaking.

Dillard's. Based in Little Rock, Arkansas, a major department store chain in the United States, with 330 stores in 29 states.

diminish. To make less or cause to appear less.

direct mail. Printed matter (such as circulars) prepared for soliciting business or contributions and mailed directly to individuals. Typically, this refers to programs in which entire databases are mailed with a particular offer.

disagreeable. Can describe a person who is able to disagree with the acceptable norm or social considerations.

discipline. To train or develop by instruction and exercise, especially in terms of self-control.

dissertation. An extended, usually written treatment of a subject.

Dollar Store. A variety store or price-point retailer that sells inexpensive items, usually with a single price point for all items in the store. Typical merchandise includes cleaning supplies, toys, and confectionary. Typically serves communities too small for Wal-Mart.

dominate. To take over, overpower, or bring into submission of another or others.

do nots. A made-up word; things a person wants to avoid or not do.

double down. Term from the game blackjack whereby a person doubles up a previous bet in hopes of either doubling his or her winnings or making up losses.

downside. A negative aspect; worst-case scenario.

downturn. A downward turn, especially toward a decline in business and economic activity.

earn. (1) To become duly worthy of or entitled or suited to; (2) to make worthy of or obtain (e.g., *earn* your business).

economic contraction. A shrinking or lessening relating to or based on the production, distribution, and consumption of goods and services.

economy. The structure or conditions relating to or based on the production, distribution, and consumption of goods and services in a country, area, or period. A country, company, and even an individual has an economy.

effective. Producing a decided, decisive, or desired effect.

elated. Marked by high spirits; exultant.

encourage. To give help or patronage to (e.g., *encourage* others to do business with you).

end all. Describes the ultimate solution.

endurance. The ability to withstand hardship or adversity, especially the ability to sustain a prolonged stressful effort or activity.

enlist. To secure the support and aid of; employ in advancing an interest.

entrée. The main course of a meal.

environment. The circumstances, objects, or conditions that surround a person.

erode. To cause to deteriorate or disappear as if by eating or wearing away.

exception. A case to which a rule does not apply.

exhibit. To present to view, as in showing or displaying outwardly, especially by visible signs or actions.

expand. To increase the extent, number, volume, or scope of; enlarge (comes from *spread*).

expansion. Act of increasing the extent, number, volume, or scope of; enlargement.

experience. (1) Direct observation of or participation in events as a basis of knowledge; (2) the fact or state of having been affected by or gained knowledge through direct observation or participation.

exploit. (1) To make productive use of; utilize; (2) to make use of meanly or unfairly for one's own advantage.

extra mile. More than is due, usual, or necessary.

extraordinary. Anything outside the realm of what most normal people can and do achieve.

fanatic. Marked by excessive enthusiasm and often intense uncritical devotion.

financial plan. A plan of how to stay solvent with regard to income and expenses.

first quarter. The first three months of a financial year.

flier. An advertising circular.

Fortune 500. Top 500 companies in the United States based on gross sales.

freelancer. A person who pursues a profession without a long-term commitment to any one employer.

front. An area of activity or interest.

fuel. Support; stimulate.

funk. Slump.

GDP (Gross Domestic Product). One of the measures of national income and output for a given country's economy.

It is the total value of all final goods and services produced in a particular economy—the dollar value of all goods and services produced within a country's borders in a given year.

generate. To create or be the cause of (a situation, action, or state of mind).

genuine. Free from hypocrisy or pretense; sincere.

goals. The end toward which effort is directed.

Greece (ancient). Considered to be the foundation of Western civilization, as a golden age flourished in this culture for many generations. When the Romans conquered Greece, they adopted many aspects of this culture. Roman civilization in turn went on to conquer much of the world and so spread Greek culture to many other countries.

guarantee. An assurance for the fulfillment of a condition such as an agreement by which one person undertakes to secure another in the possession or enjoyment of something.

gullible. Easily duped or cheated.

hammer. To strike or drive with a force suggesting a hammer blow or repeated blows.

Heard Automotive. Founded by Bill Heard, who operated the largest Chevrolet franchise in the world and who closed all operations in 2009.

HerbaLife. Founded in 1980, a company that sells weight-loss, nutrition, and skin care products by multilevel marketing, also known as network marketing. It has been the subject of controversy and lawsuits.

high-handed. Having or showing no regard for the rights, concerns, or feelings of others.

high margin. A product or service that has a high difference between its cost and its selling price.

hot stuff. Someone or something unusually good.

Howard Schultz. Born July 19, 1953, Schultz is an American businessman and entrepreneur best known as the chairman and CEO of Starbucks and a former owner of the Seattle SuperSonics.

huddle. (1) To gather in a close-packed group; (2) to curl up; (3) to hold a consultation.

hungry. (1) Eager; avid (e.g., *hungry* for affection); (2) strongly motivated (as by ambition).

information-assisted selling. Using information to help the consumer and the overall sales process so that it is quick and easy.

insane. Absurd; extreme.

instructional. The action, practice, or profession of teaching (e.g., *instructional* videos).

intensity. The quality or state of being intense, especially an extreme degree of strength, force, energy, or feeling.

invest. To involve or engage, especially emotionally (e.g., *invest* time and energy).

iPod. A brand of portable media players designed and marketed by Apple Inc. and launched on October 23, 2001.

irrational. Not governed by or according to reason; without reason. This is used in the good sense of irrational (e.g., Be *irrational* in the level of actions you are willing to take in order to realize your dreams).

Jesus Christ. Jesus of Nazareth, the son of Mary; source of the Christian religion and savior in the Christian faith.

knock off. The act of discontinuing some activity that is unwanted or unproductive.

know. (1) To perceive directly; have direct cognition of; (2) to have understanding of; to recognize the nature of; to discern; to recognize as being the same as something previously known; (3) to be acquainted or familiar with; (4) to have experience of; to be aware of the truth or factuality of; to be convinced or certain of; to have a practical understanding of.

knowledge. The fact or condition of knowing something with familiarity gained through experience or association; acquaintance with or understanding of a science, art, or technique; the fact or condition of being aware of something; the range of one's information or understanding.

lack. To be short of or have need of something.

lazy. (1) Not inclined to activity or exertion; not energetic or vigorous; (2) encouraging inactivity or indolence.

liability. An action causing a person to be exposed or subjected to some usually adverse contingency or action.

lifestyle. The typical way of life of an individual, group, or culture.

literature. (1) The body of writings on a particular subject (e.g., scientific *literature*); (2) printed matter (e.g., leaflets or circulars).

locked up. Unable to shift; fixed.

logical. (1) Of, relating to, involving, or being in accordance with logic; (2) skilled in logic; (3) formally true or valid; analytic; deductive.

long recession. A recession that lasts longer than the average length of 18 months.

magnify. To enlarge in fact or in appearance.

mantra. A commonly repeated word or phrase.

market share. The percentage of the market for a product or service that a company supplies.

marketing campaigns. A connected series of operations designed to promote, sell, and distribute a product or service.

marketplace. The world of trade or economic activity; the everyday world.

Mary Kay. A brand of skin care and color cosmetics sold by Mary Kay Inc. Mary Kay World Headquarters is located in Addison, Texas, a Dallas suburb. Mary Kay Ash founded Mary Kay Inc. on Friday, September 13, 1963. Richard Rogers, Mary Kay's son, is chairman and CEO, and David Holl is president and COO.

misnomer. A wrong or inappropriate name or designation.

MLM (multilevel marketing). Also known as network marketing, a marketing strategy that compensates promoters of direct-selling companies not only for product sales they personally generate but also for the sales of others they introduced to the company. The products and company are usually marketed directly to consumers and potential business partners by means of relationship referrals and word-of-mouth marketing.

momentum. Strength or force gained by motion or through the development of events.

money. Something generally accepted as a medium of exchange, a measure of value, or a means of payment, such as officially coined or stamped currency.

motives. Something (e.g., a need or desire) that causes a person to act.

movers and shakers. Refers to people who make things happen.

must. (1) To be commanded or requested to (e.g., you *must* stop); (2) be urged to; ought by all means to.

myth. An unfounded or false notion.

necessity level. (1) The magnitude of the pressure of circumstance; something that is necessary in relation; requirement; (2) an urgent need or desire; the magnitude of a quantity considered in relation to an arbitrary reference value.

negativity. (1) Lacking positive qualities; especially disagreeable; (2) marked by features of hostility, withdrawal, or pessimism that hinder or oppose constructive treatment or development; (3) promoting a person or cause by criticizing or attacking the competition.

negotiate. To confer with another so as to arrive at the settlement of some matter. (*Note from the author:* Although most believe that *negotiate* means to accept a lower price, negotiating has nothing to do with discounting the price of your product or service.)

neurochemistry. The study of the chemical makeup and activities of nervous tissue.

newsletter. A small publication (such as a leaflet or newspaper) containing news of interest chiefly to a special group.

norm. A principle of right action binding upon the members of a group and serving to guide, control, or regulate proper and acceptable behavior.

nurture. To further the development of; foster.

NuSkin. An American direct-selling company that sells cosmetics, nutritional supplements, and technology services. It was founded by Nedra Dee Roney and Blake M. Roney in 1984 and was officially listed on the New York Stock Exchange under the ticker symbol NUS in 1996.

objection. (1) A reason or argument presented in opposition; (2) a feeling or expression of disapproval.

occupancy. The fact or condition of being occupied or lived in.

offset. Something that serves to counterbalance or compensate for something else, especially either of two balancing ledger items (e.g., *offset* the pullback).

old school. Something not updated; a way of thinking that is not necessarily wrong but is not current.

oops. Used typically to express mild apology, surprise, or dismay.

opportunities. (1) A favorable juncture of circumstances; (2) a good chance for advancement or progress.

overtly. Open to view; manifest

participate. (1) To take part; (2) to have a part or share in something.

passive. (1) Receiving or enduring without resistance; submissive; (2) existing or occurring without being active, open, or direct; (3) relating to or being in a business activity in which the investor does not actively participate in the generation of income.

peddle. (1) To sell or offer for sale from place to place; (2) to deal out or seek to disseminate; (3) to offer or promote as valuable.

Peninsula Hotel. An ultra-luxury hotel operator based in Hong Kong. Its flagship hotel, the famous Peninsula Hong Kong, which opened in 1928, used to be known as the "finest hotel east of the Suez" and is probably one of the best hotels in the world.

perfect. To make perfect; improve or refine.

pinned down. Unable to move.

playtime. A time for play or diversion.

positive. (1) Having a good effect; favorable (e.g., a *positive* role model); (2) marked by optimism (e.g., the *positive* point of view).

power base. The starting point or line for an action or undertaking whereby a person has possession of control, authority, or influence over others. Military term meaning a place where military operations begin.

PR (public relations). The business of inducing the public to have understanding for and goodwill toward a person, firm, or institution; also the degree of understanding and goodwill achieved.

PR campaign. A connected series of operations designed to bring about a particular result; in this case, inducing the public to have understanding for and goodwill toward a person, firm, or institution.

price sensitive. Having or showing concern for something specific, in this case, price.

prima donna. A vain or undisciplined person who finds it difficult to work under direction or as part of a team.

problems. (1) A source of perplexity, distress, or vexation; (2) difficulty in understanding or accepting; (3) opposition to a solution.

produce. (1) To compose, create, or bring out by intellectual or physical effort, (2) to bear, make, or yield something.

product. Something (such as a service) that is marketed or sold as a commodity.

production. In terms of personal production, the total results of a person's efforts.

product line. Group of products manufactured by a firm that are closely related in use and production and marketing requirements.

profit. The excess of returns over expenditure in a transaction or series of transactions; especially the excess of the selling price of goods over their cost.

profitable. Affording profits; yielding advantageous returns or results.

programmed. To predetermine the thinking, behavior, or operations of as if by computer.

proposition. Something offered for consideration or acceptance; proposal.

prosper. (1) To succeed in an enterprise or activity; especially to achieve economic success; (2) to become strong and flourishing.

protocol. A code prescribing strict adherence to correct etiquette and precedence.

psychological. The mental or behavioral characteristics of an individual or group.

psychosomatic. Of the mind.

public office. A position, elected or appointed, in which governmental functions are exercised.

pullback. Reversal in growth.

pundit. A person who gives opinions in an authoritative manner, usually through the mass media.

purpose. (1) Something set up as an object or end to be attained; an intention; (2) resolution; determination.

qualify. To declare competent or adequate. In sales, it means determining a person's financial ability.

quantities. A considerable amount or number.

quarter. One of four three-month divisions in a year.

quest. An act or instance of seeking; a pursuit or search.

quit. (1) To cease normal, expected, or necessary action; (2) to give up employment; (3) to admit defeat; to give up.

quitter. One who quits; especially one who gives up too easily; defeatist.

rail. To revile or scold in harsh, insolent, or abusive language.

rant. To talk in a noisy, excited, or declamatory manner.

ravings. Irrational, incoherent, wild, or extravagant utterances or declamations.

Ray Kroc. (October 5, 1902–January 14, 1984). Took over the (at the time) small-scale McDonald's Corporation franchise in 1954 and built it into the most successful fast-food operation in the world. Kroc was included in *Time 100: The Most Important People of the Century* and amassed a $500 million fortune during his lifetime. He was also the owner of the San Diego Padres baseball team starting in 1974.

reactivate. To make active again.

reactive. Occurring as a result of stress or emotional upset (not in a good sense).

reasonable. (1) Being in accordance with reason (a *reasonable* theory); (2) not extreme or excessive.

recession. Period of general economic decline, usually defined as a contraction in the GDP for six months (two consecutive quarters) or longer. Marked by high unemployment, stagnant wages, and a fall in retail sales. A recession generally does not last longer than one year and is much milder than a depression. Although recessions are considered a normal part of a capitalist economy, there is no unanimity among economists as to their causes.

referral. The act, action, or an instance of referring.

relationship. (1) The relation connecting or binding participants in a relationship; (2) a specific instance or type of kinship.

reluctance. Feeling or showing aversion, hesitation, or unwillingness.

repackage. To package again or anew; specifically, to put into a more efficient or attractive form.

resistance. An opposing or retarding force.

response. Something constituting a reply or a reaction.

restrict. To confine within bounds; restrain.

restrictions. Something that restricts, such as a regulation that restricts or restrains.

résumé. A document that contains a summary or listing of a person's relevant job experience and education. The résumé or CV (curriculum vitae) is typically the first item that a potential employer encounters regarding a job seeker and is typically used to screen applicants. An application screening is often followed by an interview. (Don't ever rely on a résumé without taking the time to meet the person who you want to hire.)

revenue. The total income produced by a given source.

revitalize. To give new life or vigor to.

ridicule. Implies a deliberate, often malicious, belittling.

rocket ride. An experience because of actions taken that would be like rapid travel, as if in a rocket.

Rotary Club. An organization of service clubs located all over the world. It is a secular organization open to all persons regardless of race, color, creed, or political preference. There are more than 32,000 clubs and more than 1.2 million members worldwide. The members of Rotary Clubs are known as Rotarians. The stated purpose of the organization is to bring together business and professional leaders to provide humanitarian service, encourage high ethical standards in all vocations, and help build goodwill and peace in the world. Members usually meet weekly for breakfast, lunch, or dinner, which is a social event as well as an opportunity to organize work on their service goals.

Rules of Success. Educational program developed by Grant Cardone that states the basic laws and actions required to create success and is delivered on CD or DVD.

sale. Contract involving transfer of the possession and ownership (title) of a good or property or the entitlement to a service in exchange for money or value. Essential elements that must be present in a valid sale are (a) competence of both the buyer and seller to enter into a contract, (b) mutual agreement on the terms of exchange, (c) a thing capable of being transferred, and (d) a consideration in money (or its equivalent) paid or promised.

schedule. Timetable for a program or project showing how activities and milestone events are sequenced and phased over the allotted period.

second money. Money that comes from a second sale.

second sale. A sale made after the first sale as an addition to the first purchase. This is not to be confused with the next time a person sells to someone.

selective. (1) The act of being judicious or restrictive in choice; discriminating; (2) highly specific in activity.

selling. Considered by many to be a sort of persuasive "art." Contrary to popular belief, the methodological approach of selling refers to a *systematic process of repetitive and measurable milestones by which a salesperson relates his or her offering of a product or service, in return enabling the buyer to achieve his or her goal in an economic way.* In business, "nothing happens until someone sells something."

sensory. Of or relating to sensation or to the senses.

service. Contribution to the welfare of others. The act of serving is a helpful act or is useful labor that does not produce a tangible commodity but benefits all parties involved in some way.

shameless. (1) Having no shame; insensible to disgrace; (2) without a painful emotion caused by consciousness of guilt, shortcoming, or impropriety. (This is a good thing in this context.)

shock. (1) A sudden or violent mental or emotional disturbance; (2) something that causes such disturbance (e.g., the loss came as a *shock*); (3) a state of being so disturbed.

shortcut. A method or means of doing something more directly and quickly than, and often not so thoroughly as, by ordinary procedure (not a good thing).

skill. (1) The ability to use one's knowledge effectively and readily in execution or performance, dexterity, or coordination, especially in the execution of learned physical tasks; (2) a learned power of doing something competently; (3) a developed aptitude or ability.

snob. (1) One who tends to rebuff, avoid, or ignore those regarded as inferior; (2) one who has an offensive air of superiority in matters of knowledge or taste.

socialized. The process of learning one's culture and how to live within it (not a good thing in this context).

social networking. Online communities of people who share interests and/or activities or who are interested in exploring the interests and activities of others. Most social network services are Web-based and provide a variety of ways for users to interact, such as by e-mail and instant messaging.

social norms. A principle of right action binding upon the members of a group and serving to guide, control, or regulate proper and acceptable behavior.

Social Security. Primarily a social insurance program providing social protection or protection against socially recognized conditions, including poverty, old age, disability, unemployment, and others.

society. A group of humans characterized by patterns of relationships between individuals who share a distinctive culture or institutions.

soft economy. An economy that is lacking robust strength, stamina, or endurance.

solicit. To try to obtain, usually by urgent requests or pleas.

solution. (1) An action or process of solving a problem; (2) an answer to a problem.

spend. (1) To pay money, usually in exchange for goods or services; (2) to use a resource, such as time.

sphere of influence. The area in which an individual has the power to act or produce an effect without apparent exertion of force or direct exercise of command, usually due to a relationship, authority, or reputation.

stall. To hold off, divert, or delay by evasion or deception.

standards. Something set up and established by authority as a rule for the measure of quantity, weight, extent, value, or quality.

Steve Jobs. Cofounder and CEO of Apple.

stream. (1) A steady succession (as in words or events); (2) a constantly renewed or steady supply.

success. Attaining a target or targets that a person has set for him- or herself. According to this author, there are three factors to success: it is important, it is your obligation, and there can never be a shortage of it.

sufficient. Enough to meet the needs of a situation or a proposed end.

sum total. Total result; totality.

superfreak. An ardent enthusiast to an excessive degree; someone who goes all the way!

supplier. External entity that supplies relatively common, off-the-shelf, or standard goods or services, as opposed to a contractor or subcontractor who commonly adds specialized input to deliverables. Also called *vendor.*

suppress. (1) To put down by authority or force; (2) subdue; to restrain from a usual course or action; (3) to inhibit the growth or development of.

surrounding agreement. The thinking and ideas of the group or environment around a person.

survey. (1) The act of examining as to condition, situation, value, or appraisal; (2) act of querying in order to collect data for the analysis of some aspect of a group or area.

survive. (1) To remain alive or in existence; to live on; (2) to continue to function or prosper. (Most people think of just getting by, but that is not the definition used here.)

swing for the fences. Baseball jargon suggesting trying to hit a home run. In business, it means that a person really went for it.

target. That which a person is trying to accomplish.

Ten Commandments. A list of religious and moral imperatives that, according to Judeo-Christian tradition, were authored by God and given to Moses on Mount Sinai (Exodus 19:23) or Horeb (Deuteronomy 5:2) in the form of two stone tablets. They feature prominently in Judaism and Christianity.

ten times. Multiplied results by the number 10.

therein. In that particular respect (e.g., *therein* lies the problem).

thrive. (1) To grow vigorously; flourish; (2) to gain in wealth or possessions; prosper; (3) to progress toward or realize a goal despite of or because of circumstances.

tight. Characterized by firmness or strictness in control or application or in attention to details (e.g., a *tight* schedule).

top dog. A person, group, or thing in a position of authority, especially through victory in a hard-fought competition.

toxin. A poisonous substance that is a specific product of the metabolic activities of a living organism and is usually very unstable, notably toxic when introduced into the tissues, and typically capable of inducing antibody formation.

training. (1) The act, process, or method of one who trains; (2) the skill, knowledge, or experience acquired by one who trains.

unemployment rate. Percentage of the total workforce who are unemployed and are looking for a paid job. Unemployment rate is one of the most closely watched statistics because a rising rate is seen as a sign of a weakening economy that may call for a cut in interest rates. Likewise, a falling unemployment rate indicates a growing economy, which is usually accompanied by a higher inflation rate and may call for an increase in interest rates.

unique. (1) Being without a like or equal; unequaled; (2) distinctively characteristic.

unwavering. (1) Not vacillating between choices; (2) not fluctuating in opinion, allegiance, or direction.

value. Relative worth, utility, or importance.

value-add. Creation of a competitive advantage by bundling, combining, or packaging features and benefits that result in greater customer acceptance.

value proposition. Mix of goods and services and price and payment terms offered by a firm to its customers.

vein. A bed of useful mineral matter.

vendors. Manufacturer, producer, or seller.

verbalize. To express something in words.

Vikings. Norse traders and adventurers who ruled the seas in Medieval times but whose culture and activities died out during the expansion of the Christian world.

Vince Lombardi. (June 11, 1913–September 3, 1970). He was the head coach of the Green Bay Packers of the NFL from 1959 to 1967, winning five league championships during his nine years. Following a one-year retirement from coaching in 1968, he returned as head coach of the Washington Redskins for the 1969 season.

Wachovia Bank. Based in Charlotte, North Carolina, a diversified, wholly owned financial services subsidiary of Wells Fargo. Wachovia Corporation was purchased by Wells Fargo on December 31, 2008, and it ceased to be an independent corporation on that date. Over the next three years, the Wachovia brand absorbed into the Wells Fargo brand. Wachovia Corporation's stock was traded on the New York Stock Exchange under the ticker WB.

Wall Street. A 1987 film about a young stockbroker who forms an apprenticeship with an immoral corporate raider.

Wal-Mart. An American public corporation that runs a chain of large discount department stores. It is the world's largest public corporation by revenue, according to the 2008 Fortune Global 500. Founded by Sam Walton in 1962, it was incorporated on October 31, 1969, and listed on the New York Stock Exchange in 1972. It is the largest private employer in the world and the third-largest utility or commercial employer.

warning. (1) The act of giving admonishing advice to; counsel; (2) act of calling one's attention to or informing.

Warren Buffet. The most successful investor in the world. From humble beginnings, he worked a paper route and sold newspapers door to door. Now he is ranked in the top five of the world's wealthiest people.

Washington Mutual (WaMu). A savings bank holding company and the former owner of Washington Mutual Bank, which was the United States' largest savings and loan association. On September 25, 2008, the U.S. Office of Thrift Supervision (OTS) seized Washington Mutual Bank from Washington Mutual Inc. and placed it into the receivership of the Federal Deposit Insurance Corporation (FDIC). The OTS took the action due to the withdrawal of $16.4 billion in deposits during a 10-day bank run on June 30, 2008.

wealth. (1) Tangible or intangible thing that makes a person, family, or group better off; (2) abundance of valuable material possessions or resources.

willing. (1) Inclined or favorably disposed in mind; (2) prompted to act or respond.

word-of-mouth. Generated from or reliant on oral publicity.

World Trade Center. Sometimes referred to as WTC or Twin Towers. A complex in Lower Manhattan whose seven buildings were destroyed in 2001 in the September 11 attacks. The site is currently being rebuilt with six new skyscrapers and a memorial to the casualties of the attacks.

wow. Used to express strong feeling (as in pleasure or surprise).

Xbox. Video game console produced by Microsoft Corporation. It was Microsoft's first foray into the gaming console market and competed with Sony's PlayStation 2 and Nintendo's GameCube. The integrated Xbox Live service allows players to compete online.

zombie. A person who resembles the so-called walking dead.

About the Author

Grant Cardone is a *New York Times* best-selling author and internationally recognized sales training expert. He is seen regularly on CNBC, MSNBC, Fox News, and Fox Business. He is also a contributor for the *Huffington Post*. Joan Rivers recently did a segment on him and his family on her show, "How Did You Get So Rich?"

Mr. Cardone has been working with companies worldwide for 25 years, customizing and providing sales programs and systems to improve sales processes and increase sales revenues. He has spoken to audiences in every major city in the United States and Canada, Brazil, the Caribbean, Austria, England, and Australia. His methodologies are being employed in businesses in Ireland, Russia, Taiwan, and as far away as Kazakhstan. His books are being translated into multiple languages including German and Chinese. He developed a virtual on-demand sales training site for the automobile industry (www.salestrainingvt.com) and is releasing a similar site for individuals and other sales organizations (www.cardoneuniversity.com).

Audiences travel from all around the world to attend his one-day live seminars. His first book, *Sell to Survive*, reached the top 1 percent of self-published books and is considered "the definitive book on selling for the twenty-first century." One reader said, "The information in *Sell to Survive* is the first new thing written on selling in 50 years!" Another stated, "After reading sales books for years, this book stands above every other book I have ever read on this topic." His first published book, *If You're Not First, You're Last*, recently became a *New York Times* best-seller.

Mr. Cardone has also proven himself off the stage, in the real world of business. He owns three successful companies that were all started from just an idea and with no money, just hard work.

In addition to his entrepreneurial undertakings, Mr. Cardone is heavily involved in philanthropic activities and has been acknowledged by the U.S. Senate, Congress, the mayor of Los Angeles, and others. He was recently awarded the Rajiv Gandhi Award for his efforts in bringing Indian and American businesses together and the Distinguished Alumni Award from McNeese State College, where he received his accounting degree.

Mr. Cardone resides in Los Angeles with wife, actress and producer Elena Lyons, and their daughter, Sabrina Francesca.

Index